THE A. S. W. ROSENBACH FELLOWSHIP
IN BIBLIOGRAPHY

AN
AMERICAN
BOOKSHELF
1755

PUBLICATIONS OF THE ROSENBACH FELLOWSHIP
IN BIBLIOGRAPHY

I

PROPOSALS RELATING TO THE EDUCATION OF YOUTH
IN PENSILVANIA
By
Benjamin Franklin

II

EX LIBRIS CARISSIMIS
By
Christopher Morley

III

AN AMERICAN BOOKSHELF 1755
By
Lawrence C. Wroth

AN

AMERICAN

BOOKSHELF

1755

By

LAWRENCE C. WROTH

Librarian

THE JOHN CARTER BROWN LIBRARY

Rosenbach Fellow in Bibliography

PHILADELPHIA:

UNIVERSITY OF PENNSYLVANIA PRESS

London: Humphrey Milford

Oxford University Press

1934

To

BARBARA PEASE WROTH

In 1930 Dr. A. S. W. Rosenbach founded at the University of Pennsylvania a Fellowship in Bibliography. Dr. Lawrence C. Wroth, Librarian of the John Carter Brown Library and President of the Bibliographical Society of America, was the holder of the Fellowship in 1932–33. The present volume contains the three lectures which he delivered at the University in the spring of 1933, supplemented by notes and a bibliographical appendix.

ACKNOWLEDGMENT

IT seems sometimes that the moment of greatest satisfaction in the making of a book, the moment least al-
loyed by nagging doubts and fears, is that in which one
reviews the contributions that others have made to the ad-
vancement of his task, and because in the present case it
has not always been possible to make specific acknowledgment in the text and notes of such contributions, I gratefully name here those to whom I am particularly indebted
for aid and encouragement: Messrs. A. S. W. Rosenbach,
Verner W. Crane, George Simpson Eddy, Clarence Saun-
ders Brigham, Alexander J. Wall, Austin K. Gray, Robert
W. G. Vail, C. Seymour Thompson, George S. Godard,
William Smith Mason, Leonard L. Mackall, Wymberley
W. De Renne, Benjamin C. Nangle, Lathrop C. Harper,
Ernest Spofford, Julius H. Tuttle, L. Nelson Nichols,
Otis G. Hammond, and George Parker Winship. I owe
thanks also to various members of the staffs of the Library
of Congress, the American Antiquarian Society, the Ameri-
can Philosophical Society, the New York Historical Society, the Library of Yale University, the John Hay Li-
brary of Brown University, and the Providence Public
Library. Special acknowledgment is due to my associates in
the John Carter Brown Library—Miss Catherine C.
Quinn and Miss Marion W. Adams.

L. C. W.

CONTENTS

AN AMERICAN BOOKSHELF 1755

INTRODUCTION

AS a preliminary to the examination we shall be making
of certain selected books and pamphlets issued in and
about the year 1755, I should like to introduce to you Mr.
James Loveday, a merchant of Philadelphia whose circumstances made possible an indulgence of more than common
degree in the habit of reading, and, I should like to add,
whose predilections led him naturally to reflection upon
the men and events of his American world. James Loveday was born in 1720. Soon after coming of age, he inher-
ited his father's house and mercantile business, and in the
decade that followed became by the grace of his own industry a man of varied and substantial interests whose
ideas and opinions counted more than a little in his active
community. Until the Revolution forced him to choose between his native land and a country he revered, Mr. Loveday walked among the conservatives in the field of politics.
He supported the Proprietary right in Pennsylvania, and,
except when the Navigation Acts and certain vexatious customs regulations restricted too narrowly the movements of
his ships, he stood firmly behind the administrative measures of the royal government. It is not easy to define his
religious affiliations and beliefs, but judging from an expressed dislike of Presbyterianism, regular and New Light,
of Methodism, and of nonconforming sects in general, including the Quakerism that surrounded him, I am led to
believe that he adhered, without excess of zeal, to the
middle way of the Church of England.

Loveday's affairs carried him frequently from his cen-
trally located province into several neighboring colonies;
his correspondence brought him into relationship with
busy, alert men of his own kind in every American city

from Boston to Savannah. Wherever he went in the course of his journeys, he was notable even among his well-informed associates for a persistent patronage of the booksellers. Observing this characteristic, it soon became a matter of routine with his correspondents to keep him supplied with the important issues of their local presses. Many a pamphlet of distant origin that otherwise he would never have seen came his way along with the prices current, the advertisements, and the long, gossipy trade letters sent him by merchants of New England, New York, and the South. He read these pamphlets, and he read also the newspapers, the periodicals, and the occasional issues of the native press; that is, its broadsides, its sheet ballads, and even its advertising handbills. He was unlike most of his contemporaries, furthermore, in that he preserved in order and seemliness the ephemeral printed matter that came to him from these scattered sources, leaving to us through his respect for the printed word a record of his time in such degree as the features of those troubled years revealed themselves in print.

But this description of the attributes of Mr. Loveday must come to an end before I find myself believing too completely in my evocation of him. My purpose in these lectures is not a projection of the ideal, but a study of the actual as it existed in colonial America in a specific period of time. To carry out this study I propose examining a group of writings that any American of the decade 1750–1760 might have been familiar with if he had been so happily placed in the circumstances of life, so catholic in his tastes, so industrious in the acquisition of books, and so assiduous in the reading of them as this hypothetical individual whom I have brought into being for our convenience.

It need not be objected against this creature of the imagination that, in the mock-Dundrearian phrase, "no fellah ever saw such a fellah," because no fellah claims that he did. Nor need the construction of a figure so ideal disturb the logician, for I shall not be trying to prove anything upon the basis of its characteristics. Mr. Loveday serves simply as a funnel through which will pour for our ease in examination the printed matter of several communities. No thesis underlies this review of the books of 1755, unless it be one of that sort known in the cant of the schools as a "fact-finding" thesis. We are interested in books, and we are interested in our fathers. We want to know what ideas stirred in their minds in this restless period in which began the downfall of the colonial system and the making of a nation, this period that we now recognize as presaging also the end of an economic stage in human society. We should be able to learn something of the nature of these ideas by running through the current printed matter in various fields that came to James Loveday's table from the presses of Philadelphia and other American cities, and from the presses of London over the counters of Franklin & Hall and their rivals among the Philadelphia booksellers of his day. We shall be taking for granted Loveday's general literary background, assuming that he maintained his reading of the Latin classics, the early English poets, and the writings of Mr. Addison and Mr. Pope and their contemporaries. What interests us in his reading rather than these factors common in our experience and in his, are the books of his time that have passed out of general knowledge, the current flow that provided him recreation and kept him in touch with the thought and doing of his American contemporaries.

In the year 1755, there were twenty-four presses in operation in fifteen towns of ten of the English American colonies. If their ephemera are counted, the output of these presses was very much greater than is shown by even so broadly conceived a list of publications as the *American Bibliography* of Charles Evans, for calculations that need not be repeated here suggest that where one title of the period has been recorded 4.7 pieces were actually printed.[1] On that basis we may think of the publications of the year 1755 as numbering at least 1,200 titles instead of the 257 recorded by Mr. Evans. There is no greater mistake possible than for the student of literature to assume that this production of the native press is beneath his notice, to say in his haste that it consists of little save almanacs, chapbooks, sermons, assembly documents, and thin imitations of contemporary English *belles lettres*. This American writing, of which only the outstanding specimens have yet been carefully studied, presents, on the contrary, a varied, even a rich, assortment of literary forms. It reveals to the diligent student a quality of style and a degree of worth in matter that are commanding increased respect from scholars as the years go by. There does not emerge from it, truly enough, the title of a single memorable work of imaginative literature. That finer gift of the human spirit was to be made only when daily living had taken on a more tranquil aspect. But in this writing that found publication through the dingy colonial printing shops there was an abundance of clear thinking and vigorous expression in the realms of politics, religion, philosophy, and science. From these presses came also a conventional and mannered literary product that was acceptable to contemporary readers of taste and sophistication; and from them came at the same time a racier literature that emerged from the land itself and was formed by the conditions confronting the men who inhabited it. Despite the meagerness of their harvest, the colonial American writers succeeded in keeping the field of letters under cultivation, passing on to their nineteenth-century successors the legacy of a soil that had been ploughed for generations and nourished by the chemistry of continuous effort.

In the first of the lectures I am privileged to give upon this Rosenbach Foundation that promises so much for the future of bibliography and literary history in America, I shall confine myself to discussing a group of writings that had their origin in the troubled politics of the decade 1750–1760. As the course proceeds I plan to talk about the writings on the other subjects I have mentioned, hoping that in the end we shall have acquired something like a picture of our Mr. Loveday's mind, and so, of the mind of his friends and associates throughout the colonies. I should like to be able to convince you by this procedure that the historian of a movement, the Revolution, let us say, who studies only the political writings of the period preceding it does not learn what manner of men they were who made the Revolution; that it is essential to know what problems of the inner life these men had encountered; what new visions were opening to their view; what old theories they had discarded in the realms of science and economics; what their experience had been in the literature of fancy; what they knew of history and of current ideas; and what were their hopes for the future of the life about them. I believe we do not understand these men unless some such projection of their consciousness has been made upon ours, and, lacking that projection, we do not wholly understand the movements they initiated and carried through. And I see no way to gain a comprehension of these intellectual and emotional experiences of our fathers except by studying the product of their contemporary press. The history of a period and its writings are one, and there exists in abundance material to enliven and enrich our conception of both American history and American literature. We have lost something in having been taught, and in teaching others in our turn, that American history is one thing and American literature a thing apart that began to stammer its way to a hearing only in the early years of the nineteenth century. Despite the assertion made a moment ago, it may be that, after all, a thesis, or at least a purpose, underlies this examination of the books of 1755.

I

POLITICS AND PROPAGANDA

BECAUSE of its exceptional interest in the history of the American colonies, I have chosen 1755 as the central year of our examination. I have allowed myself leeway in the matter of consistency by placing above and below Mr. Loveday's shelf of 1755 other shelves from which I may draw at will books of earlier and later years of the decade whenever a relationship of purpose or matter seems to make inescapable the discussion of them in connection with the books of the chosen year.

THE DIFFUSION OF PRINTING

There occurred in Boston in the year 1754 an incident in the history of the American press that Loveday found himself reading about with something more than curiosity when a pamphlet of the next year setting forth one side of the story came to his table. He had previously read with some amusement a Boston tract of 1754, entitled *The Monster of Monsters*, an extraordinarily witty satire, issued without name of place or printer under the pseudonym, "Thomas Thumb, Esq."' He had almost forgotten its mockery of the deliberations in the Massachusetts Assembly upon a proposed excise act when repercussions of its local effect reached him in the form of a pamphlet of 1755, entitled *A Total Eclipse of Liberty*,³ in which the Boston printer Daniel Fowle angrily related the story of the irregular trial before the Assembly which followed his arrest upon the charge of having printed Mr. Thomas Thumb's satirical piece. As the result of this trial, the offending pamphlet was ordered to be burned by the hangman, and Fowle was jailed, reprimanded, and condemned to pay the costs of the proceedings. Loveday was not much surprised when he read in Fowle's *Appendix to the Late Total Eclipse of Liberty*,[4] issued in 1756, that the printer was taking his press and his outraged feelings away from a city in which the freedom of the press had been subjected to handling as rough as that meted it in this affair of the Tom Thumb pamphlet.[5] It seemed to him that the Zenger case in New York some twenty years earlier had been fought and won in vain.[6] This reflection was to come to him again two years later when the Pennsylvania Lower House defended itself with extraordinary rigor against Justice William Moore and Provost William Smith, accused of publishing matter inimical to the authority of that Assembly.[7] If he had carried his reflections to the point of seeking information on the history of press censorship in America, he would have found that never had the freedom of the press been violated in the English colonies at the initiation of King or Parliament, but that in the many remembered cases of prosecution of printers the complainants were assemblies, governors, or the people themselves acting under the warrant of mob law.

In the fall of 1756 our Philadelphian learned through the medium of a newspaper prospectus that Fowle had removed to Portsmouth, New Hampshire, and by his settlement there had established the first press of that colony.[8] Knowing well the impermanency of journalistic projects of the time, Loveday thought of the proposed *New Hampshire Gazette* as simply another newspaper of uncertain hold upon existence. He could not be expected to foresee the present moment when that journal is issued daily after nearly two hundred years of life, the oldest newspaper in continuous existence in the United States.[9]

New Hampshire was not the only colony in which occurred events of moment in typographical history in these years, but in the case of the others there were no attendant circumstances of an unusual or picturesque nature. In the spring of 1755, James Parker began at New Haven *The Connecticut Gazette*,[10] the first newspaper to be published in Connecticut despite the fact that the other functions of the press had been in continuous operation in that colony since its establishment at New London by Thomas Short in 1709.[11] The publisher of the new journal was a New Jersey man who had formerly been a journeyman of William Bradford of New York. With the aid of active partners, he was able so to expand his business as to carry on printing establishments simultaneously in three places. Well established in New York, he set up a New Haven office in 1754,[12] and in the same year by beginning printing in Woodbridge, New Jersey, he gave his native colony its first permanent press.[13] In 1761, James Adams went from the shop of Franklin & Hall in Philadelphia to establish in Wilmington the first Delaware press;[14] and in 1762, James Johnston emigrated from Great Britain to Savannah, Georgia, where he set up the first press to be operated in the newest of the colonies.[15] With the establishment of Johnston in Savannah was completed the slow process through which, beginning at Cambridge, Massachusetts, in 1639, the printing press had been located in all the thirteen original colonies.

The motive that underlay the establishment of these American presses was utilitarian, for the publication of polite literature formed a relatively small factor in the plans of the colonial printer. The government work, blank forms, advertisements, small jobs, almanacs, newspapers, and manuals of daily usefulness were the types of production he looked to for his living. Sermons, political treatises, elegies, and occasional publications arising from the aspirations of amateur men of letters added irregularly to the profit of the printer, but it was in very few instances that we find a printer deliberately entered upon a program of publishing works of purely literary interest, or even works of history with their secondary interest as literature. None the less the desire for expression forced its way through the indifference of the press, and a respectable list of works of a less utilitarian character than those by which the printer made his living came through the years from the colonial printing houses. It is this product that is to interest us chiefly in the examination of Mr. Loveday's bookshelves.

THE INDIAN IN COLONIAL POLITICS

In reading the titles of the writings that came to Mr. Loveday's table in the years of our interest we perceive how strongly enforced upon his consciousness must have been the figure that lurked and watched behind the outer settlements of all the colonies. As the balance of power between English and French, English and Spanish, French and Spanish, the Indian had always taken a large place in the thoughts and plans of Americans of all nationalities, but at no time and under no circumstances was his rôle more important or his conduct in it of greater concern to colonists than it was to the British and French between 1750 and 1763. The chief evidence of this interest on the English side appears in the existence of that long series of printed documents containing minutes of treaty conferences between the races which are known to modern bookmen as the Indian Treaties. At another time we shall be looking at the Treaties as literature;[16] our present interest in them is as one of the records of the tedious and complicated political situation from which they emerged. Innumerable journals of conferences, or treaties, went into the archives of the colonies concerned in their making and remained there in manuscript form until the universal publication of colonial records in the nineteenth century brought them again into view. We are concerned now, however, only with such Treaties as were considered sufficiently important, or of sufficient timeliness of interest, to require contemporary publication in print. Between 1750 and 1770 Loveday acquired and read seven Treaties issued by Franklin & Hall and fifteen others by various printing houses in Philadelphia, New York, Boston, London, and other cities. This average of one printed Treaty a year indicates to some degree the weight of the Indian in the thoughts and plans of the colonial American.[17] Before the publication in London in 1756 of *An Account of the Treaties between Sir William Johnson and [various] Indian Nations in 1755 and 1756*,[18] Loveday had learned from other sources the principal results of the negotiations recorded in those minutes. Reading in the printed book the detailed account of the conferences, he realized anew the wisdom and importance of the recent royal action, so long desired by many in the colonies, through which unity of control in Indian relations, for the middle colonies at least, had been secured.[19] And in common with many he was more than pleased that the office of His Majesty's Superintendent of Indian Affairs had gone to Sir William Johnson, an Irish gentleman by birth and a Mohawk by adoption, of whom Cadwallader Colden had recently written that in addition to energy, intelligence, tact, and other implied qualifications, he had "something in his natural temper suited to the Indian humour."[20] It amused Loveday a little that in spite of the presence in the colonies of so much local and imported military talent, the only victory of consequence for the English in those early years of the war, the Battle of Lake George, had been won by the civilian Sir William who, it was constantly being said by way of reproach, was without military experience.

The question of the allegiance of the Indians was always in the minds of governors and officials of the colonies from 1750 to the close of the Revolutionary War. There existed then, as later in our history, the habit of saying that the only good Indian is a dead Indian, but weighing against that dictum of mischievous and careless men were the reiterated efforts of intelligent writers and officials to reconcile the interests of two alien races occupying the same soil. As early as 1727, and at various times since in successive editions, the *History of the Five Nations* of Cadwallader Colden had stated the terms of that problem and placed it before thinking men for their consideration.[21] Nor were there lacking thinking men to attempt its solution. In 1751, Loveday was impressed by the earnestness and good sense he found set forth in a tract issued anonymously in New York in that year, and reprinted in London in 1752. He learned later that this plea for a confederacy of the colonies, for the establishment of a barrier colony, and for the adoption of a definite, unified Indian policy, this earnest appeal called *The Importance of Gaining the Friendship of the Indians to the British Interest*,[22] was from the pen of Archibald Kennedy, receiver-general of the Province of New York.[23] Kennedy was a Scotchman of the noble house of Cassilis, whose son later came into the family title. Upon his first coming to America about the year 1710, the elder Archibald Kennedy had served in the field with and against the Indian.[24] Now between his sixty-fifth and seventieth years he recorded in a series of tracts the ripened reflections of a life and occupation from which the racial problem had never been far removed. His formula for its solution omits no factor in the British interest, but it is based upon the integers of sympathy for the Indian and decent treatment of him as neighbor in peace and ally in war.

Appended to Kennedy's tract was published an unsigned letter addressed to James Parker, printer of the book, in which having expressed approval of its proposals, the writer passed on to make more specific its suggestions for a defensive union of the colonies. In this letter tò the printer and in Kennedy's suggestions are seen a prefiguring of that celebrated "Plan of Union" which Benjamin Franklin was later to propose to the country through the action of the Albany Congress of 1754, and from different sources we learn, as Loveday suspected at the time, that Franklin himself was the anonymous author of the letter.[25] Writing to Cadwallader Colden shortly before the publication of his proposals, Kennedy had confided his hope that this pamphlet containing what he modestly called "some confused ideas of Indian affairs" would be printed in time to influence the Grand Congress to be held at Albany in June, 1751.[26] Colden's own approval of these "confused ideas" is sufficiently indicated by his employment of many of them in a report on "The present state of the Indian affairs with the British, & French Colonies in North America" which four months later he drew up for the information of Governor Clinton of New York.[27] One does not know how far the Kennedy book influenced the Congress of 1751 but that question, after all, is of little pertinence, for it is certain that the ideas of its two authors prevailed effectually at the greatly more important Congress of three years later. Reading the tract and letter of 1751, one's attention is held by their advocacy of principles that afterwards provided the foundation of the "Plan of Union" of 1754. We are too apt to take literally that passage in the *Autobiography* in which Franklin wrote: "In our way thither [*i.e.*, Albany], I projected and drew a plan for the union of all the colonies under one government. . . ."[28] Instead of a scheme projected and drawn up at the eleventh hour in June, 1754, it is clear from his letter in the Kennedy book that Franklin had been cogitating the main features of his celebrated "Plan" since March, 1751, and that these features were found also, in germ, in the Kennedy essay to which the letter was attached.

The ideas put before the country by the Albany Congress of 1754 are not attributable, indeed, to individual authors.[8a] The questions involved were in the air that thoughtful men were breathing in those years, and if I say that I find the influence of Kennedy in the "Representation of the State of the Colonies," drawn up at the Congress by Thomas Hutchinson, and in the "Plan of Union" presented by Franklin, I mean only that I find in his tract of 1751 a clear statement of the general ideas underlying these chief proceedings of the Congress. Franklin recorded his reliance upon Kennedy's advice in forming the "Plan of Union" in a sentence from the *Autobiography* that follows the words quoted above: "As we pass'd thro' New York," he wrote, "I had there shown my project to Mr. James Alexander and Mr. Kennedy, two gentlemen of great knowledge in public affairs, and, being fortified by their approbation, I ventur'd to lay it before the Congress."[9]

Soon after the conclusion of the Congress in July, 1754, a pamphlet entitled *Serious Considerations on the present state of the Northern Colonies* was issued from the New York press of James Parker without name of author on the title-page. From a London edition of the tract, presumably of the same year, Loveday learned that this piece, too, had been composed by Archibald Kennedy.[30] In its text he found repeated the vigorous plea for unity and the proposals for considerate treatment of the Indians that had distinguished his tract of three years earlier. Although it had been written during the sessions of the Albany Congress, this plea was addressed to the colonial assemblies rather than to the Congress, urging for the sake of the country acquiescence in the projects for united action that might be expected to result from the deliberations then in progress at Albany. A year later, in the fall of 1755, with the Braddock defeat in every one's mind, and with the failure of the Plan of Union a certainty, another anonymous tract came from Parker's press exhorting the colonies to union against their common enemy for the avoidance of further disaster. There is internal evidence of a very good sort for believing that Kennedy was the author also of this *Serious Advice to the Inhabitants of the Northern Colonies*,[31] a tract which seems to be unknown to historians, and which has been recorded in only one bibliography and there by an incorrect title presumably taken from a newspaper announcement of its publication. The three pieces mentioned here, an earlier mercantile tract of 1750, not published until 1765, entitled *Observations on the Importance of the Northern Colonies under Proper Regulations*,[32] and two others which we ascribe to him on evidence later to be submitted, demand from us recognition of Mr. Kennedy's pretensions to a high place among the men of the time who were working intelligently and courageously for the common good. The position was cheerfully accorded him by Loveday and many other contemporary readers of his sincere and well-informed writing.[33]

Contemporary reports of the Albany Congress of 1754 were exceedingly meager. Its recommendations were rejected so promptly by the several colonial assemblies that they ceased almost immediately to be matter of general interest. One may and does conjecture the course of history if a plan of union for the colonies had been adopted at that time under the British government instead of against it as twenty years later. Franklin at least was of the opinion in 1789 that if the Plan of 1754 had won approval from the several colonies, who thought it allowed too much to the royal prerogative, and from the King, who thought it infringed his prerogative, the Revolution might not have occurred when it did or for a century afterwards.[34] At any rate that earnest attempt at the unification of the colonies, recognized in our time as of great importance in later constitutional developments, ceased abruptly to occupy the American mind. On this account there would probably have occurred no contemporary publication of the acts of the Congress if a local political enmity had not driven one of the Rhode Island delegates, Stephen Hopkins,[35] to print the chief proceedings in a pamphlet designed to explain the Plan to the people and to defend his action in voting for it. *A True Representation of the Plan formed at Albany*,[36] with date March 29, 1755, was not written in advocacy of a scheme already in limbo. It was simply a full presentation of the minutes of the Congress, omitting the Indian conferences, made to prevent further misrepresentation of that body and of its chief Rhode Island delegate. Hopkins's tract was immediately replied to in *A Short Reply to Mr. Stephen Hopkins's Vindication*.[37] The author of this production expressed pretty well the contemporary opinion of the Plan, but even better his personal and party animosity against Mr. Hopkins. His pseudonym, Philolethes, hid him so thoroughly that his identity has never been discovered, and for all the good his tract accomplished it might as well have never been published. Despite its well-timed appearance in the midst of an election campaign, Stephen Hopkins was returned governor of the colony.

The ill-management of the Indians and the consequent weakening of the British position complained of by many publicists of the time formed the burden of a Pennsylvania book of 1759 that was in actual fact an attack upon the Proprietary government of that province, but there is no doubt that this book, written by Loveday's acquaintance, Charles Thomson, Latin master of the Friends School of Philadelphia, must be regarded as something more than an arrow loosed in a local skirmish. Some two years before its anonymous publication in London in 1759, the author of this *Enquiry into the Causes of the Alienation of the Delaware and Shawanese Indians from the British Interest*[38] had been adopted by the Delaware Indians and given a name that means "One Who Speaks Truth." The future secretary of the Continental Congress began in 1757 his public career as clerk in treaty conferences to the Delaware chieftain Teedyuscung, that wise, crafty, witty, and notably alcoholic patriot who fought for years the battle of his people against the colonists on the one side and the dominant Six Nations on the other. Thomson's sympathies were passionately engaged by the plight of his adoptive nation. The emotion that underlay his attack upon what seemed to him an intolerable condition gave sincerity to the book containing it, but it was emotion controlled and directed that informed the writing of its cool, documented, relentless narrative.

We are too much accustomed to take a book for granted, to regard it as an isolated phenomenon, existing of its own right without relation to other books and things. Thomson's *Enquiry* stands as a fine illustration of the interrelation of books, movements, men, and motives. Its origin goes back to the humanitarian motive of the Friendly Association, a Quaker organization formed to urge fair and just examination of the Indian claims. The *Address*[39] of this body to Governor Denny lets us see that an inquiry into the relations of the Province with the Indians was set afoot by it as the result of irritation at the government's delays and suspicion of the official intentions toward the Indians. As that inquiry proceeded it provided the grounds of a local political issue in which the Assembly and the Friendly Association aligned themselves against the Governor and the Proprietors. Charles Thomson was the agent of the Friendly Association in its investigation, and when his *Enquiry into the Alienation of the Indians* was completed, the manuscript found its way into the hands of Benjamin Franklin, who was then in London striving to discredit the Penn administration of the Province. Recognizing immediately the value of the *Enquiry* in his campaign, Franklin took it upon himself to publish and distribute the book. An attack upon the Proprietors that implied their obstinacy and selfishness as the chief reasons for the failure of the British arms and for the consequent devastation of the frontiers of the Middle Colonies could be depended upon to stir up questions in England, and that is exactly what the book accomplished.[40]

The most spectacular charge brought against the Penns in the *Enquiry* was that which had to do with the celebrated "Walking Purchase" of 1737, a piece of excessive shrewdness on the part of the Proprietors' agents that was comparable in effect to the famous ox-hide grant of Carthage which used, in the reading of it, to lighten our struggle with the Virgilian epic. That Thomson's aim was good in recording this and other Proprietary dealings with the Delawares becomes apparent from a glance at the John Carter Brown copy of his book, a tall, uncut copy, formerly the property of Thomas Penn himself. In its margins, the harassed Proprietor has recorded denial of many statements, and angry protest against the partisan interpretation of certain facts. Franklin wrote home that it was said the Proprietor was contemplating an answer to Thomson's charges, but so far as is known his intentions never got beyond the stage of exasperated annotation of the margins of his personal copy of the *Enquiry*.[41]

With the idea of giving something of a popular character to Thomson's book, Franklin, in editing it, had added an appendix containing the *Journal of Christian Frederick Post in his Journey from Philadelphia to the Ohio.* The conservative Mr. Loveday was one of many contemporary readers who turned with relief from Thomson's contemptuous accusations against the Penns to the narrative of heroism, wisdom, and understanding that makes Post's *Journal* one of the most heartening documents remaining from the period. The success of the Moravian missionary's efforts to keep the Ohio Indians neutral during General Forbes's expedition against Fort Duquesne in 1758 has not been lost upon the historian of events in anything like the same degree that the splendid literary quality and lofty courage of his narrative have been overlooked by the historian of letters.[42]

It is easy enough to guess the reception of Thomson's *Enquiry* in Pennsylvania, where the alignment on the questions at issue between the popular and the court parties was by the time of its appearance pretty well determined. It is more interesting to learn the effect of the book upon the English readers whom it was hoped to influence by its revelations. The writer who discussed it in the *Monthly Review*[43] intimated very subtly that his opinions on the Pennsylvania dispute had been formed by reading the *Brief State* and *Brief View*[44] of the Province published in 1755 and 1756 respectively, but that the *Enquiry* and the *Historical Review of the Government of Pennsylvania*,[45] lately received, were contributing to change his views to such an extent that he was now in favor of the plan advocated by "moderate men of both parties"; that is, that the King should take over the Province and administer it as a royal government. The sentiments of this writer, who was, indeed, Ralph Griffiths, the editor of the famous *Monthly*, were so pat to the purpose for which Mr. Franklin was working in London that he had reason to congratulate himself upon the effectiveness of his printed propaganda.

It would be possible to speak at much greater length of the books relating to the Indians that came into Loveday's hands, but already it may seem to you that I have given them space out of proportion to their importance. But keeping in mind that we are trying to learn the fabric of our forefathers' consciousness in this period, it does not seem that I have dwelt too insistently upon the books relating to the Indian affairs. To us, the Indian is a ghost that has faded from the scene. To James Loveday and the men of his time, the Indian, when not in the same street, was always just around the corner, and, unless kept in a state of friendliness, always ready for the display of shrewd and sudden mischief.

THE REPLY TO THE FRENCH ENCROACHMENT

Discussion of writings about the Indians leads easily enough to consideration of the political propaganda which preceded and carried through the period of the French and Indian War. The dynastic problems underlying the Seven Years' War in Europe found little attention paid them by the American press, for from New England to Georgia, the colonies were thinking of only one thing. French aggressiveness in America had been a vague bugaboo, a piece of the perennial Indian and Jesuit bogey, until Céleron de Bienville actually entered the Ohio Valley in 1749 and planted his leaden plates at the mouths of the Ohio tributaries. Then a species of claustrophobia attacked the inhabitants of a group of colonies shut in on the north by the Lakes and the St. Lawrence, on the west by the Alleghanies, on the south by the Spanish settlements of Florida. The plans of the great land companies and those of private men in need of land alike were set awry by the news of the Céleron de Bienville expedition. In 1750, we find land companies and provinces sending out surveyors and marking roads; in 1751, Franklin was writing his essay on the *Increase of Mankind*, and Kennedy was giving expression to the prevailing fears regarding constriction of the country's territories. The French encroachment was now upon every man's lips.

The publication in Williamsburg in 1754 of Washington's *Journal* of his embassy to the French at Fort Le-Boeuf in the last months of the preceding year brought the issue squarely and with specific instance before thinking men throughout the country. In this unimaginative book was perceived the thing itself, the "encirclement policy" in action, and throughout the colonies could almost be heard the click with which the bald fact was received into the collective mind. Incidentally this little book, longed for by the bookman, and longed for in vain in these later years,[46] was Washington's introduction to his countrymen outside Virginia. Reading that straightforward narrative of a drama enacted against the background of a gloomy forest, men everywhere recognized the sagacity of an untried youth who perilously delayed his mission that he might carry with him Indian leaders willing to lay down the treaty belts previously received from the French. His name was already known through this adventure and through his misfortune at Fort Necessity, when its fame was added to by his conduct in Braddock's campaign, from which he alone came out with advanced reputation. Doubtless our Mr. Loveday was one of those Christopher Gist had been visiting when some months after the disaster of Braddock's defeat he wrote to Washington from Philadelphia: "Your name is more talked of in Pennsylvania than that of any other person in the army, and every body seems willing to venture under your command. Mr. Franklin . . . told me that if you would write a pressing letter desiring assistance [of the Assembly] you would get it sooner than anyone in America." About this time, Loveday read a Virginia sermon printed in Philadelphia in 1755, entitled *Religion and Patriotism the Constituents of a Good Soldier,*[47] in which the Rev. Samuel Davies, in a true spirit of prophecy, suggested in a footnote that "that heroic youth, Col Washington" had been divinely sent for the present and future good of his country. It is doubtful whether the English readers of the London edition of the *Journal* were definitely impressed by this name sounding unexpectedly from the western wilderness, but when the French in 1756 had issued their *Mémoire contenant le Précis des Faits*,[48] designed to show that it was this same Washington's killing of Jumonville in the Fort Necessity campaign, among other offensive actions enumerated, which had begun the war (O tempora! O mores!), they had more reason to keep in their memories a name the world was never again to forget. Loveday read this *Mémoire* in the French and in the translation published by James Chattin in Philadelphia in 1757.[49] He also saw copies, all in this year, of the same translation in two New York editions, published by Hugh Gaine[50] and Parker & Weyman,[51] and extracts from it published in the Dublin edition of William Livingston's *Review of the Military Operations*.[52] He wondered somewhat at the ways of Destiny as he saw a great reputation looming through defeat and disaster in the field,[53] and taking form in the very face of a charge of assassination brought by a European power of the first class.

It was during the first year of the War that printed pieces of the kind we now designate as propaganda began to pour in almost daily upon Loveday's library table. One of the earliest of these to come to him in 1755 was the anonymous *State of the British and French Colonies in North America*,[54] printed in London early in the year. This dispassionate statement of the British case, in spite of its firmness, failed to please the extremists, for, as happens always in periods of this kind, it had become unfashionable to allow the enemy any rights whatever. The tract seems to have been published while John Huske, a New Englander then resident in London, was writing his notable book on the same subject, and to have added fuel to the

fire of anger which that writer maintained against the
French. ". . . this very Week," wrote Huske, "a Pamphlet has been published, called the *State of the British
and French Colonies, &c.* which accuses his *Majesty's*
Colonies with committing Frauds, Abuses, Encroachments,
Murders, and every species of Villainy, against the poor
Indians of *North-America,* by which they have been alien-
ated from, and induced to take up Arms with the *French*
against, Us; and all the Evils *America* labours under have
been thus produced." In succeeding pages, Huske bears
hard upon this string of criticism, though he concedes that
the author of the book he thus condemned "wrote with a
View to inform and serve his Country." As one accustomed
to weigh arguments and evidence, however, Loveday
found himself better pleased with the calm analysis of the
anonymous writer of the *State of the Colonies* than with
Huske's more popular whooping-on of the dogs of war.[55]
He was in agreement, indeed, with an English reviewer
who wrote appreciatively of the former tract and on the
same page ironically praised Huske's performance and
promised the gratitude of the English people for others
like it on the ground that their publication would increase
the consumption of paper, "now become a considerable
article in the British manufactory."[56]

Loveday's opinion of the Huske pamphlet was not so
fixed in distaste as to prevent his realizing that it was the
most effective of all the tracts of the period in arousing
and forming popular opinion. *The Present State of North
America, &c. Part I,*[57] was indeed a clear, vigorous, and
incisive attack upon the French pretensions, telling its
readers exactly what they wished to be told and omitting
to remind them of unpleasant truths. It was published in
two editions in London in 1755, and in the same year it
appeared in Dublin and in two issues in Boston. In translation it formed the larger part of a German compilation of

Frankfurt, 1755, the *Allgemeine Amerikanische Kriegs-geschichte*. The continuation of the *Present State*, containing chapters IV–VIII, seems never to have been published, though when the second edition of Part I was printed, its author still expected to bring out Part II. In a note at the end of that edition of the book, he wrote as follows: "The rest of this Work will be published with all possible dispatch, with an accurate Map of the Country, shewing the Rights of Great Britain, France, and Spain." But there is no record of his publication of Part II. It is probable that by this time the war, now well under way, needed no additional aid from his pen, or it may be that the author had been discouraged from further public expression of his opinions by the mockery of Part I just quoted from the pages of the *Monthly Review*. The only part of his promise fulfilled in print was that which related to the map. It may be remarked by way of a librarian's jest that the vociferous writer of this book belied the name under which his work is erroneously entered in the catalogue of a famous library. He was anything in characteristics but a member of the "Hushe" family.

When Loveday read the brief notice of the *Present State* in the *Gentleman's Magazine* for May, 1755,[58] he was puzzled by the reviewer's assertion that the tract was chiefly drawn from Butel-Dumont's *Histoire et Commerce des Colonies Angloises*[59] of Paris, 1755. He would have been even more astonished if he had lived to our own day and found one bibliographer after another repeating that unfounded statement.[60] Butel-Dumont's book was a cool, informative work, with an inevitable French bias, as different as possible from Huske's angry denunciation of French policy in America. Even the superficial resemblance to be expected between any two works on the same general subject fails to manifest itself in face of the radical difference in purpose between these respective statements of the French and English claims.

In spite of the irony expressed by the *Monthly Review* at the expense of Mr. Huske, the eight editions and issues of his tract published in two years indicate its unusual popularity—perhaps the greatest degree of that factor attained by any of the books mentioned in this examination.[61] The chauvinism of its matter that gave offence to Loveday seems to have been acceptable to most of his countrymen. Even so sober a writer as Dr. William Clarke refers to Huske's book in his *Observations on the Conduct of the French*[62] as "wrote with the greatest Perspicuity, Judgment and Spirit, (for which every Englishman is greatly obliged to the ingenious Author) . . ." Ten years later, the doctor's fellow citizens of Boston forgot this service rendered the common cause by Mr. Huske, their former townsman, when it was reported to them that it was his suggestion which had led to the imposition of the Parliamentary Stamp Act. Between the burning of Huske in effigy on Boston Common in 1765 as the consequence of that report and his friendly coöperation with Franklin in his famous testimony before Parliament on the Stamp Act[63] in 1766 lies a vale of inconsistency on the part of Huske or of misunderstanding on the part of his contemporaries that historians are now trying to explore.

Before the year was out, Loveday began to feel a bit wearied by the unchanging note of the books that came from the English and American presses. William Clarke's *Observations on the Conduct of the French*,[64] Boston, 1755, was little more than a competent synthesis. It held unusual interest for Loveday, however, because appended to it was Franklin's anonymous essay on the *Increase of Mankind*, a piece, afterwards acknowledged by its writer, which began with general scientific reasonings and became in the end another specific attack upon the French policy.

In that essay, originally written in 1751, but not then published, he found matter of particular local interest in its author's expostulation against the invasion of Pennsylvania by Germans of the Palatinate, who, retaining their language and customs, failed to assimilate with the English-speaking colonists and remained a dangerous foreign unit of population. Here was an early protest, put forward with acrimony, against the efficacy of the "melting-pot" theory. Several years later, in 1754, Franklin published his *Memorial of the Case of the German Emigrants*[65] in which he made constructive suggestions towards the process known in our day as the "Americanization" of these people who had settled themselves firmly in Pennsylvania, and in the rich valleys of Maryland and Virginia. One might suppose that the publication in 1755 of a piece in which the German inhabitants of Pennsylvania were described as "Palatine Boors" would have proved embarrassing to the author of the *Memorial* of 1754, especially as that author was at the time a trustee of the Society for Propagating Christian Knowledge among the Germans settled in Pennsylvania. In October of 1755, however, Franklin sent a copy of Dr. Clarke's pamphlet to his London correspondent, William Strahan, and, without comment upon its anti-German sentiments, called attention to his own part of the production.[66] It is said, however, that before this time Colden and Alexander had criticized the expression of these sentiments in letters to their author, and it is certain that in later printings of the *Increase of Mankind*, in 1760 and 1769, the offending sections were omitted from the text.[67] Other writers of the time animadverted upon the German invasion so often and so bitterly that reading their words one realizes the extent and antiquity in our land of the problem of immigration.

More than once in these early days of the war Loveday had occasion to reflect upon the absence of harmony between the Middle Colonies and New England, each with its ideas as to the importance of its relative field of action, each liable to break out in recrimination of the other's policies and leaders. The two tracts attributed to the Rev. Charles Chauncy, the *Letter to a Friend*, and the *Second Letter to a Friend*,[68] of Boston, 1755 and 1756, he regarded as salt in the wounds left unhealed after the Braddock campaign. He resented, too, the schoolmasterly attitude of Dr. Chauncy, and felt that the lesson of his tracts might have been better received if their writer had known more intimately the internal political conditions of the Middle Colonies. And particularly did he resent the complacent assertion by Dr. Chauncy of the superior military ability of the ordinary New England citizen as compared to the man of the Middle and Southern colonies.

GOVERNMENT AND OPPOSITION IN THE MIDDLE COLONIES

Throughout the period of the French war, almost every one of the colonies was the seat of internal political conflicts between governor and assembly. The same presses that urged the claims of empire brought out various tracts that appeared on both sides of a disintegrating struggle which prevented the full coördination of colonial effort in the war. In another sense, however, these struggles were the opposite of disintegrating in character. In them the leaders of the people received a training in resistance to authority which enabled the country in 1765 to oppose with success the operation of the Stamp Act, and from their printed literature the people themselves received instruction in the principles and theories of citizenship that prepared them for the test of 1776. In 1755 appeared in London a pamphlet in behalf of the Proprietary interest in Pennsylvania, attacking the Quaker party in the Assembly of that Province and accusing that party, among other things, of exploiting the German residents for its political ends. Those who maintained that the colonies had "invited the Calamities they suffer," wrote John Huske, ". . . had support in their Clamours from a late Pamphlet called a *Brief State of the Province of Pennsylvania*, which I shall say no more of at present than that it is calculated for private Purposes, at the Expence of a very respectable Body of People called *Quakers*, to whom this Country is more obliged than most People at present know or can imagine, and who will very soon be acquited, with Honour, of the exceptionable Conduct laid to their Charge." The author of this *Brief State of the Province of Pennsylvania*,[69] published anonymously in two editions of London, 1755, and a third of 1756, was almost certainly the Rev. William Smith, Provost of the College of Philadelphia, though soon after the publication of the book Franklin wrote Collinson that he did not believe "our Friend Smith" had had any hand in its composition, but that the piece had come from the governor himself.[70] Franklin came to see before long that he had been mistaken in his exoneration of Smith from what he deemed an offensive charge. In later years he accepted the general attribution to Smith of this tract which the Assembly party pretended to despise, but which nevertheless its supporters took great pains to refute. *An Answer to an Invidious Pamphlet entitled a Brief State*[71] asserted that the author of the "invidious Pamphlet" was "very well known to be a Smith," and proceeded to give him a character for iniquity that we know was undeserved.[72] One wonders whether this *Answer*, said to have been composed by a "Mr. Cross," was the vindication that Huske seems to suggest was in preparation when he was writing the words just quoted from his *Present State*. Dr. Smith replied to the *Answer* with his longer and weightier *Brief View of the Conduct of Pennsylvania*.[73] The forthright tone of his attack upon the popular party is exemplified in this sentence from one of the early pages of that book. "Before I conclude," he wrote, "I shall fully prove against the Assembly, that it is not libelling of them, to say that they are a factious Cabal, effectually promoting the French Interest, and a dead Weight upon his Majesty's Service." It is no wonder that the Assembly three years later took advantage of a political misstep by Dr. Smith to lay him away in quod, denying him the privilege of *habeas corpus* and compelling him by the imprisonment of his person, to conduct the classes of this University, then in its tender infancy, in the common jail of Philadelphia. As the result of a voyage to England and a personal representation to the legal and administrative authorities of the kingdom, Dr. Smith had the rich satisfaction of returning to Philadelphia in 1759 bearing a rebuke addressed by the Privy Council to the Assembly for the measures taken against him two years before.[74] In the meantime there appeared in Philadelphia, in 1759, a second reply to his anti-Assembly pamphlets, and though the author of the new attack spoke of them disdainfully, his refutation was nearly twice as long as both of Dr. Smith's pieces together. This *True and Impartial State of the Province of Pennsylvania* has been attributed to Franklin, but aside from the matter of style that leads one in the first instance to question the attribution, and aside from the fact that earlier in the same year Franklin had been responsible for the publication in London of a more elaborate book of the same tenor, the famous *Historical Review of the Government of Pennsylvania,* there exists evidence in an unpublished letter of William Franklin's which shows conclusively enough that its author was the Maryland-Pennsylvania politician and man of affairs, Joseph Galloway.[75]

From the New York press of James Parker came in 1752 *An Essay on the Government of the Colonies,*[76] an anonymous, well-written little work, by one who acknowledged himself a "governor's man" and defended vigorously the government of New York against the Assembly of that colony. This tract possesses far more than local interest, for its writer laid down the extreme constitutional theory that the colonies existed as fiefs of the Crown, permitted to meet in Assembly not by right but by the royal grace. The argument was firmly and skilfully put, and the book would doubtless be mentioned more often by historians if more historians knew of it. It is not in the bibliographies, however, and I have seen only a single copy of it in the libraries. Though it must have stung the colonial liberals wherever it went, the memory of its attitude seems to be preserved by only a single contemporary reference. William Smith, Jr., cites it in a note to his *History of New York,* and quotes from it a passage in which the writer, advising the assemblies "to drop those parliamentary airs and style about liberty and property, and keep within their sphere," expressed with more than usual straightforwardness the stricter government point of view as opposed to the theory of the colonials that they were "entitled to all the privileges of Englishmen." "It is easy to conceive," wrote Smith, "that contentions must naturally attend such a contradiction of sentiments."[77] A further distinction in the history of ideas in America possessed by this *Essay* lies in its plain declaration that the colonies as crown domains were not within the authority of Parliament. When Richard Bland of Virginia promulgated what has been described as "the startling doctrine that the British colonies in America were united to the empire only through the British crown, and not at all through the British Parliament,"[78] he nowhere stated his case more succinctly than had been done some fourteen years earlier by the author of the *Essay* in these words: "We are Parcel of the Dominions of the Crown of England; we are no Part, nor ever were, of the Realm of England, but a peculiar of the Crown; and by a natural and necessary Consequence, exempted from parliamentary Aids."[79] In reading Bland's *Inquiry into the Rights of the British Colonies,*[80] of Williamsburg, 1766, with the anonymous *Essay* by its side, one feels that the Virginia writer had not been far from a copy of the New York production during the composition of his own tract. The double edge of the blade of argument used in the two books manifests itself in the manner the weapon was employed by the respective authors: the author of the *Essay* made use of it to defend the royal prerogative against the assemblies, the author of the *Inquiry* as a weapon to support the disobedience to Parliament of the American people in the Stamp Act controversy.[81] One looks about hopefully for the writer of this early statement of a constitutional principle of which so much was to be heard in later years, but as no obvious candidates for the honor of its authorship present themselves, we are led by reason of its general tenor and of certain specific ideas found in its pages to suggest that it was one of the series of anonymous political writings that came in this period from the pen of Archibald Kennedy.[82]

THE CLERGY AS PROPAGANDISTS

If anyone in these years had told Loveday that the clergy were losing their influence in public life, he would have pointed rather sardonically to the sermons of the year 1755 in which the war against Catholic France was preached as a holy crusade by the ministers of several denominations. The Rev. Samuel Davies, who became president of Princeton in 1759, preached in the years of the war at least six sermons of a patriotic tenor. In Maryland the Rev. James Sterling, at Governor Sharpe's instance, addressed the Assembly, urging the members in the names of Religion and Patriotism to awaken to their responsibility in the prosecution of the war. Originally published in Annapolis at the public charge,[83] his sermon, which was really an elaborate political tract, was reprinted in London with the title *Zeal against the Enemies of our Country pathetically recommended*. Mr. Sterling had published three years earlier a long and somewhat grandiose poem, in which under the innocent title *An Epistle to the Hon. Arthur Dobbs*,[84] he had sung the battle song of British imperialism. In later years his poems on various subjects were to become well known to the Philadelphia literati through their publication in Dr. William Smith's *American Magazine*. From New England came in 1755 thirteen sermons on the war addressed to public bodies and militia organizations. Church and State went hand in hand throughout the country stirring the people to resentment against the French policy, and as usual the sins of the Scarlet Woman gave the clerical writers excuse for a deal of invective.

THE MAP AS A POLITICAL FORCE

One of the charges against the French that Loveday found repeated insistently in the writings of the American and English publicists was that they were deliberately revising their maps in this period to show boundaries which confined the English colonies to the narrow Atlantic seaboard between Florida and Nova Scotia. "Boastful," "impudent," "lying," were a few of the adjectives applied to the French cartographical policy. The maps of Bellin, De Lisle, and DeFer were selected for particular vilification. William Smith, Jr., in his *History of New York* recorded that Bellin, the French Royal Hydrographer, had said cynically to Governor Shirley, in discussing this matter of the changes in the maps, that in France one followed the royal commands.[85] Looking upon these maps of the period when the French encirclement policy was in the actual stage of execution, one can understand the indignation aroused in Loveday and his contemporaries by their visual representation of the French claims, by what seems their graphic expression of contempt for the English pretensions. The colonials longed for maps which should show the English side of the argument. In 1755, two productions that seemed sent in answer to their desires appeared respectively in London and Philadelphia. These were the celebrated map of Dr. John Mitchell of Virginia and London, and that of equal fame by Lewis Evans of Philadelphia.

"The Mitchell, who made the Map, is our Dr. Mitchell," wrote Franklin to Jared Eliot,[86] who evidently had inquired if the compiler of the great eight-sheet map,[87] issued under the auspices of the Lords of Trade, were indeed the scholar and scientist, many years a resident of Virginia, who had been for so long one of that group of correspondents on natural history and science, on agriculture, mechanics, and the industrial arts that numbered Franklin, Colden, Bartram, Garden, and Eliot among its members. For some fifteen years before the publication of the map, Mitchell had been living in England. The exact nature of his occupation in those years seems to be unknown. It is on record that at one time in this period he wished to secure appointment as postmaster-general of North America, but that he gave up this idea because he was not able to assure the authorities of the income they thought should arise from the colonial postal system.[88] In spite of his relative obscurity in this period it is clear that he was in touch with some of the great men in English official life, and that his influence with them was sometimes asked by his American friends. He emerges prominently with his employment by the Lords of Trade to compile the great map published February 13, 1755, a cartographical work of the first class which was at the same time an official political document, the most important statement, indeed, of the British claims regarding America to come from a government source. It is asserted on the face of the map, over the signature of John Pownall, secretary of the Lords of Trade, that it had been compiled from original surveys in the Plantations Office, a circumstance that doubtless contributed to the favor with which it was regarded by the British government for a generation or more. Later issues of this map were used by the British and American commissioners at the Treaty of Paris in 1783, and upon the so-called "King George" copy, issue of 1775, now in the British Museum, were laid down for the first time on any map the boundaries of the new United States of America.[89] But it was not altogether its cartographical excellence that led such men as John Huske and William Smith, Jr., to praise the Mitchell map in the early years of its existence. Their admiration, to a large extent, was based upon its graphic statement of the territories that the official construction of treaties allowed the French in America. ". . . It must give every Briton great Pleasure," wrote John Huske, "to see our Countryman Dr. Mitchel . . . detecting their [*i.e.*, the French] Mistakes and designed Encroachments, and almost wholly restoring us to our just Rights and Possessions, as far as Paper will admit of it, in his most elaborate and excellent Map of North-America just published; which deserves the warmest Thanks and Countenance from every good Subject of his Majesty's Dominions."[90] Two years later the historian of New York wrote: "Dr. Mitchel's [map] is the only authentick one extant."[91]

Mitchell's picture of the British case in his map found verbal expression in a tract said to have been written by him, published anonymously in London in 1757, entitled the *Contest in America*,[92] a well-argued, factually rich assertion of the British claim to the Ohio country, based upon the existence of English settlements and trading posts in the great valley, years before the French invasion of it. The author prescribed for a boundary between the two colonial empires the natural barrier formed by the St. Lawrence and the Lakes, and believing that the great extent and varied and conflicting interest of the British colonies made impossible a union comprising all of them, he proposed a "triple union"; that is, three administrative and defensive unions made up much as are now the groups we call New England, the Middle States, and the Southern States. Loveday found himself in agreement with the commendatory notice of the *Contest* written for the *Monthly Review,* as we know today, by Oliver Goldsmith,[93] though he failed to be disturbed by, or even to notice, the "inequality of style," "want of method," and "disgusting iteration of the same observations" which offended the artistic sense of that great master of simplicity in English style.

Despite the unlooked-for notoriety they acquired in current intercolonial politics, I wish to treat the *General Map* of Lewis Evans and the two pamphlets related to it as belonging to another category than the political, as part, indeed, of the writings associated with the western expansion, then beginning, by which a new frontier was formed while the old coastal colonies were still in process of settlement. If it seems to you that these works are hardly related to the topics with which they are grouped in the next lecture, I take refuge in the device I have imagined and assert that it is in this position I find them upon Mr. Loveday's shelf.

NOTES

1. This point is discussed in L. C. Wroth, *The Colonial Printer*, pages 184–186, on the basis of a comparison between the Franklin & Hall Work Book (manuscript in the New York Public Library) and the list of titles in Campbell's *Collection of Franklin Imprints in the Museum of the Curtis Publishing Company*.

2. For full title, see Evans, No. 7332. The authorship of this tract against the Excise Bill of 1754 has been variously attributed to Benjamin Church (Sabin, No. 12982), Samuel Waterhouse (Evans, No. 7332), and Samuel Cooper. Evans records that the Boston Athenaeum copy is inscribed in a contemporary hand: "The supposed authors Benj. Brandon of Boston & Rev^d. Dr. Mayhew." This tract marked the crisis in the controversy over the Excise Act and Provincial Stamp Duty. Several other titles of 1754 appeared on one side or another of the dispute. In one of these, *The Crisis . . . Printed in June 1754*, page 16, we find "Now in the Press, and will be publish'd with all Speed. The Monster of Monsters."

3. Evans, No. 7418. The *Appendix to the Late Total Eclipse of Liberty* there entered as "second title" is also entered by Mr. Evans as No. 7664 under the year 1756, where it properly belongs.

4. Evans, No. 7664. See preceding note.

5. An account of Daniel Fowle's trial is found in Isaiah Thomas, *History of Printing in America*, I, 333–337, and the incident is discussed at length in C. A. Duniway, *The Development of the Freedom of the Press in Massachusetts*, pages 115–119.

6. Livingston Rutherfurd, *John Peter Zenger, his Press, his Trial and a Bibliography of Zenger Imprints*, New York, 1904.

7. See note 74.

8. The best discussion of the beginnings of the press in New Hampshire is in the *Proceedings of the American Antiquarian Society*, October, 1915, pages 327–330, being an addition to the Librarian's Report by Dr. Charles L. Nichols. It is to be regretted that Mr. Loveday did not preserve the prospectus of the *New Hampshire Gazette* mentioned in the foregoing text, for its existence is known today only through a reference to certain "printed Proposals," previously issued, in Fowle's address to the public in the first issue of the newspaper, October 7, 1756.

9. Clarence S. Brigham, "Bibliography of American Newspapers,

New Hampshire," in *Proceedings of the American Antiquarian Society*, April, 1916; pages 149–163. See also Evans, No. 7726.

10. *Ibid.*, "Connecticut," October, 1913; pages 291–292; and Evans, No. 7399.

11. W. De Loss Love, *Thomas Short, the first Printer of Connecticut*, page 42.

12. A succinct statement of Parker's setting up a press in New Haven, and of the later history of that press, is found in Victor Hugo Paltsits, "John Holt, Printer and Postmaster," in the *Bulletin of the New York Public Library* for September, 1920.

13. Most authorities assert that Parker established a press at Woodbridge in 1751, but no imprints are known to have come from that town until 1754. See William Nelson, "Some New Jersey Printers and Printing in the Eighteenth Century" in *Proceedings of the American Antiquarian Society*, April, 1911; and Constance H. Humphrey, "Check-List of New Jersey Imprints" in *Papers of the Bibliographical Society of America*, XXIV, 1930, Parts One and Two, pages 43–149.

14. A sketch of James Adams by Miss Dorothy L. Hawkins of the Vassar College Library has been completed and is scheduled to be read before the Bibliographical Society of America in October, 1933. A brief account of the beginnings of Delaware printing by Douglas C. McMurtrie is found in *The American Collector* for August-September, 1932, entitled "The Delaware Imprints of 1761," pages 135–137.

15. *Catalogue of the De Renne Georgia Library*, I, 145–148.

16. See Chapter III.

17. The definitive bibliography of the printed Indian Treaties is Henry F. De Puy, *A Bibliography of the English Colonial Treaties with the American Indians*, New York, 1917.

18. De Puy, work cited in preceding note, No. 34.

19. The reference is, of course, to the creation in 1756 of the office of "His Majesty's Sole Agent, and Superintendant of the Affairs of the Six Confederate Nations of Indians."

20. *Colden Papers*, IV, 277, in a report by Colden on Indian affairs of unusual interest. See note 27, below.

21. A full discussion of this important book will be found in Chapter III.

22. See Appendix I.

23. Kennedy's contemporary importance and influence at home and abroad have hardly been appreciated by modern students; see note 33, below.

24. This biographical fact is referred to in his tract on the *Importance of Gaining the Friendship of the Indians*, page 9, but it seems to have been overlooked by his biographers.

25. See Appendix I for a letter from Kennedy to Colden in which Franklin's authorship of this letter to the printer is spoken of.

26. See Appendix I where the essential part of this letter is given in full.

27. Colden to Clinton (*Colden Papers*, IV, 271–287), dated at end "New York Aug 8th 1751," headed, "The present state of the Indian affairs with the British & French Colonies in North America with some observations thereon, for securing the Fidelity of the Indians to the Crown of Great Brittain & promoting Trade among them."

28. Smyth, *Writings of Benjamin Franklin*, I, 387.

28a. For earlier proposals of plans for the union of the colonies, see note 81, below.

29. Smyth, *Writings of Benjamin Franklin*, I, 387. In the *Colden Papers*, IV, 441–444, 449–451, 459–461, 463, are several letters of Colden, Franklin, and James Alexander, written at this juncture relating to the Plan of Union.

30. See Appendix I. It should be remarked that the use of the words "Northern Colonies" in this and the following tract marks the distinction in the author's mind between the colonies of the mainland and those of the West Indies, not between the northern and southern mainland colonies.

31. Appendix I.

32. Appendix I.

33. One impressive evidence of the influence of the Kennedy tracts is found in the extent to which *The Importance of the Friendship of the Indians* and the *Serious Considerations* are drawn upon by the author of the *State of the British and French Colonies*, published in London in 1755, and by Dr. John Mitchell in his *Contest in America*, London, 1757. Doubtless other instances could be found of their influence upon contemporary writers.

34. See Smyth, *Writings of Benjamin Franklin*, III, 226–227n.

35. In "The Statesmanship of the Albany Congress," *i.e.*, Chapter VI, Part One, of *Stephen Hopkins, A Rhode Island Statesman* (Rhode Island Historical Tracts, No. 19, Parts One and Two, Providence, 1884), William E. Foster has treated the Albany Congress with a fullness and an appreciation of its importance that, I believe, has not yet been exceeded. It is strange that no one seems to have given mono-

graphic treatment to this most important of intercolonial congresses. The Albany Plan of Union is discussed, of course, in Frederick D. Stone's article on plans of union in Carson's *Historical Celebration of the Constitution of the United States*. See reference in note 81, below.

36. Evans, No. 7433; Reprinted in *Rhode Island Historical Tracts*, No. 9.

37. *A Short Reply to Mr. Stephen Hopkins's Vindication and false Reflections against the Governor and Council of the Colony of Rhode Island &c.*, signed at end "Philolethes" and dated, "Rhode-Island, April 10, 1755." "The authorship of this anonymous pamphlet still remains unsolved." (Foster, work cited in note 35 above, Part I: 186n.) This piece was reprinted in Rhode Island Historical Tracts, No. 9, pages 47–65.

38. Appendix II.

39. Appendix II.

40. Appendix II.

41. A comparison of the handwriting in the margins of this volume with that in a letter written by Thomas Penn, dated *July 25, 1759*, courteously supplied me in a photostat copy of the original by the Historical Society of Pennsylvania, makes clear the identity of the annotator. This copy of the book has written upon its fly-leaf in pencil: "The Manuscript Notes are in the autograph of Thomas Penn, son of the Founder of Pennsylvania C.W." and a query in the hand of George Parker Winship: "Note by Charles Welford (?)."

42. The two *Journals* of Post are given more extended treatment in Chapter III.

43. *Monthly Review*, June 1759, pages 545-548. I am indebted to Mr. Benjamin C. Nangle of Yale University for the knowledge that this reviewer was Ralph Griffiths, editor and publisher of the *Monthly Review*.

44. These two pamphlets will be discussed at length later in this section.

45. Though attributed to Franklin by his contemporaries and by writers for generations afterwards, it seems that his part in the production of this work was chiefly one of instigation, publication, and distribution. The history of the book may be followed in the following references: Ford, *Franklin Bibliography*, No. 253; Smyth, *Writings of Benjamin Franklin*, IV, 82; R. A. Austen Leigh, "William Strahan and his Ledgers," *The Library*, March, 1923; George Simpson Eddy, "Account Book of Benjamin Franklin, 1757–1762," in *Pennsylvania*

Magazine of History and Biography, LV, No. 2, 1931, page 121 and *note*; and William Smith Mason, "Franklin and Galloway, some Unpublished Letters," in *Proceedings of the American Antiquarian Society*, October, 1924, pages 254–255. In the passage last referred to Mr. Mason suggests Richard Jackson as the author of the *Historical Review*, an attribution in which he is supported by Mr. Eddy in two letters to me dated May 21 and 22, 1933.

46. For facsimile of title-page and full collation see *Church Catalogue*, No. 998.

47. Evans, No. 7403, where it is said that the sermon was reprinted in 1756 in both London and Glasgow. Sabin, No. 18763, records the London edition of 1756.

48. Sabin, No. 47511, records three editions, all of Paris, 1756; that is: 4to, pages vi, 198; 12mo, pages viii, 275; and 12mo, pages 292, *should be* xii, 292. In addition to these the John Carter Brown Library has these two editions: 12mo, pages viii, 54, [2], 55–70, 73–276; and 8vo, pages ii, 220. There were in 1756 and 1757 other French editions of The Hague and Paris. In 1757, the book appeared in London in an English translation entitled *The Conduct of the Late Ministry*, and again in 1759 as *The Mystery Reveal'd*. There were also three American editions of 1757. (See below, notes 49, 50, and 51.) A bibliographical study of all the original editions, and of the distinct English and American translations, is now in progress by the staff of the William L. Clements Library. The actual compilation of the *Mémoire* was entrusted by the French government to Jacob-Nicolas Moreau, afterwards historiographer of France. In his autobiography (*Mes Souvenirs*, edited by Camille Hermelin, 2 Parts, Paris, 1898–1901, Part I, pages 62–63 and *note*) is found Moreau's statement of his responsibility for the work, and a note by the editor to the effect that Moreau had preserved, and that there still existed, the bundle of documents sent him by the government as the material of his compilation. Among these was a transcript of Washington's diary of the Fort Necessity Campaign, the original of which has been lost to knowledge since the publication of the *Mémoire*.

49. Evans, No. 7897. See note 48, above.

50. Evans, No. 7896. See note 48, above.

51. Evans, No. 7895. See note 48, above.

52. This work will come in for more attention in Chapter II.

53. It seems to have proved no deterrent to the growth of Washington's reputation that John Huske, writing in 1755 in London in the

Present State of North America, page 66, should have said of his sur-
render at Fort Necessity that its Articles of Capitulation "were the
most infamous a British Subject ever put his Hand to."

54. Sabin, No. 90601. The work is cast in the form of "Two Letters to a Friend." The "Second Letter" is dated March 14, 1755, and
refers, page 141, to the *Brief State of Pennsylvania*, published in February, 1755, and as the *State of the British and French Colonies* was
noticed in the *Monthly Review* for June, 1755, it is fair to assume that
it was published in April or early in May of that year. In his *Present
State of North America*, page 41, John Huske writes ". . . this very
Week a Pamphlet has been published, called the *State of the British
and French Colonies, &c.*" In Appendix III reasons are given for believing that Huske's book was still being written late in April of 1755.
The "Second Letter" of the *State* is based upon communications from
two American correspondents. The first letter draws frequently upon
the pamphlets of Colden and of Archibald Kennedy, and the first section of the second letter contains statistics of population of the colonies
which later were summarized in the table, page 4, of the *Serious Advice
to the Inhabitants of the Northern Colonies*, New York, 1755, attributed to Archibald Kennedy. The second section of the "Second Letter" contains remarks on population based upon Franklin's "Observations upon the Increase of Mankind," though that piece was not published until some months after the *State* was in print. But Franklin had
been generous with manuscript copies of this essay: he sent a copy to
Colden on December 6, 1753 (*Colden Papers*, IV, 431) and in September of the same year Peter Collinson writes Colden of having received a copy of the little treatise among others of Franklin's writings.
(Work cited, IV, 406.) See also note 67, below.

55. In his *Discussion sommaire sur les anciennes Limites de l'Acadie*,
of Basle, 1755, the French writer Pidansat de Mairobert shows himself in agreement with Mr. Loveday on this point. "Dans cet Écrit,"
he writes, page 30, "où l'on sonne le tocsin de la guerre contre la
France, & où l'indiscrétion & la partialité ont égaré l'amour de la Patrie,
& précipité l'Auteur dans des erreurs multipliées . . ."

56. *Monthly Review*, June, 1755, pages 483–484. I am indebted to
Mr. Benjamin C. Nangle of Yale University for the information that
this reviewer was, almost certainly, Sir Tanfield Leman, Baronet.

57. An elaborate note on this book and its authorship appears in Appendix III.

58. *Gentleman's Magazine*, May, 1755, page 238.

59. *De Renne Catalogue*, I, 134. In our Appendix III is given an account of the German edition of this book of 1755 and 1756. A long review of an English edition of it, headed, by the English title of the book, "An Account of the British Trade and Settlements in North America," is found in the *Gentleman's Magazine* for May and June, 1755, pages 213–217 and 261–264, respectively.

60. This misconception of the *Present State* was perpetuated by the note in the old John Carter Brown *Catalogue*, Part III, No. 1066; and by Sabin, No. 34027. A recent bookseller's report in offering the title repeats the statement apologetically.

61. The title-page of the second Boston edition is of interest as showing contemporary appreciation of the work: "N.B. This Book has been in such great Demand, that it has had two Editions already this Year in England, and this is the second Edition in Boston. And by the best Judges of the Affairs of this Country, it is thought to be peculiarly seasonable at this Time, and is worthy the Perusal of every true Englishman."

62. A more extended account of this book follows.

63. Ford, *Franklin Bibliography*, Nos. 287–297, records eleven separate editions of the *Examination of Doctor Benjamin Franklin Relative to the Repeal of the American Stamp Act*, London, 1766, in English, French, and German, and a number of printings of it as a part of larger works.

64. Published first in Boston, 1755 (Ford, *Franklin Bibliography*, No. 87), and reprinted in London in the same year. (*Ibid.*, No. 88.) The earliest notice of publication I have found is the "Just Published" in the *Boston Weekly News-Letter* of August 21, 1755. The book is entered in Ford, *Franklin Bibliography*, under 1751, the year in which Franklin's *Observations on the Increase of Mankind* was written.

65. Sabin, No. 25554, gives full title and collation as "pages 20, 8" but does not suggest that the *Appendix to the Memorial, etc.*, comprising the additional eight pages of his collation, may have been a separate and later publication.

66. Franklin to Strahan, in Smyth, *Writings of Benjamin Franklin*, III, 287.

67. This notable essay of Franklin's is discussed and reprinted in Smyth, *Writings of Benjamin Franklin*, beginning III, 63. In the version of it published in William Clarke's *Observation, etc.* (page 13), sections 23 and 24 deal severely with the German and other foreign elements then intruding into the Pennsylvania population. The harsh

comments of section 23 and the whole of section 24 are omitted from the reprintings of the essay found in the *Interest of Great Britain considered*, London, 1760, and in the *Experiments and Observations on Electricity* of London, 1769. The first edition of the essay, found in Clarke's *Observations, etc.*, has on this account, peculiar significance. The manuscript of the essay seems to have first found its way to Boston, where Clarke lived, accompanying a letter dated August 13, 1752, addressed, in the earliest form of the letter known (see *Experiments and Observations on Electricity*, London, 1769, Letter XVII, page 195) "To Doctor ——— of Boston." Smyth, *Writings of Benjamin Franklin*, III, 95, fills in the blank with the name "John Perkins." The matter of this essay on the *Increase of Mankind* was much in Franklin's mind for several years and formed the subject of an interesting correspondence between him and Richard Jackson of London, later to be a close associate. See Franklin to Jackson, May 5, 1753 (Smyth, *Writings of Benjamin Franklin*, III, 133–141); and "R.J.Esq; of London to Benjamin Franklin, Esq; of Philadelphia," undated, but beginning with the statement that the writer had now had in his hands the *Observations on the Increase of Mankind* for three years (*Experiments and Observations on Electricity*, London, 1769, Letter XXV, page 329). Dr. Clarke's book, with Franklin's essay attached, was reprinted in London in 1755 (Sabin, No. 13471), and reviewed in the *Monthly Review* for November, 1755, page 400. In the same month the authorship of the *Observations concerning the Increase of Mankind* was made public through a somewhat mutilated printing of the essay in the *Gentleman's Magazine* for November, 1755, pages 483–485, headed "By B. Franklin, Esq; of Philadelphia."

68. These tracts are attributed by common consent to the Rev. Charles Chauncy, and are entered in [Paul Leicester Ford], *Bibliotheca Chaunciana*, Nos. 31, 32, 32*, with other editions noted. "T.W." appearing in these titles was one of Chauncy's several pseudonyms. *A Letter to a Friend*, Boston edition of 1755, is, Ford writes in his preface, the rarest of Chauncy's sixty titles. It was advertised as "This Day is Published" in the *Boston Evening Post* for September 8, 1755. *A Second Letter* was advertised in the same journal on October 13, 1755. Ford, *Bibliotheca Chaunciana*, No. 31, repeats Sabin's statement that *A Letter to a Friend* has to do with the defeat in Ohio of Colonel Washington upon whom the author lays the blame. This statement is correct only if "General Braddock" is substituted for "Colonel Washington." The author refers only in passing to Washington's defeat a

year before at Fort Necessity. The two letters were published together in London in 1755 under the title *Two Letters to a Friend on the Present Critical Conjuncture of Affairs in North America*. (Ford, No. 32*, but the pagination is [i–ii], 1–54.)

69. Wilberforce Eames gives a full description of the two London editions of 1755, the Dublin edition of 1755, the London edition of 1756, and the New York edition of 1865, in Sabin, Nos. 84589–84593.

70. See Appendix IV.

71. *An Answer to an invidious Pamphlet, intituled, A Brief State of the Province of Pennsylvania* . . . London: Printed for S. Bladon, in Pater-noster Row. MDCCLV. Entered among "Books published in May" in *Gentleman's Magazine*, May, 1755, page 239. See Sabin, No. 17666, for full title and attribution of authorship to "Mr. Cross." This reply to the *Brief State* does not seem to have been written and published at the instance of the Assembly, for in a letter to Peter Collinson of August 27, 1755 (Smyth, *Writings of Benjamin Franklin*, III, 277), Franklin wrote: "I do not find that our Assembly have any Inclination to answer the Brief State. They think it below them. Perhaps they slight it too much." The opinion of the Assembly seems later to have undergone a change. See note 75 below.

72. The life and character of the first Provost of the University of Pennsylvania are fully dealt with in the elaborate biography by his great-grandson, Horace Wemyss Smith, whose *Life and Correspondence of the Rev. William Smith, D.D.*, 2 vols., Phila., 1879–1880, is a presentation strongly affected by the natural veneration of the writer for his subject. This book is rich in documents, however, and so detailed in incident that the reader is able to form from it his own conclusion as to Dr. Smith's character.

73. See Wilberforce Eames's note in Sabin, No. 84594, for authorship.

74. This interesting and dramatic struggle is treated fully in Smith, *Life of the Rev. William Smith, D.D.*, I, 167–209.

75. Full title in Ford, *Franklin Bibliography*, No. 261. For discussion of authorship, and corrected pagination, see Appendix V.

76. See Appendix I for full title and discussion.

77. William Smith, Jr., *The History of the Province of New-York*, London, 1757, page 241 and note.

78. Moses Coit Tyler, *The Literary History of the American Revolution*, I, 229.

79. This question of parliamentary jurisdiction as viewed by American publicists is admirably discussed by Randolph G. Adams in his *Political Ideas of the American Revolution*, throughout, but especially Chapters II and V.

80. Evans, No. 10244. Sabin, No. 5860, records a London edition of 1769. In 1922, the William Parks Club of Richmond, Virginia, issued as its Publication No. 1, a reprint of the original Williamsburg edition of this book, edited by Earl Gregg Swem of William and Mary College.

81. The satisfaction of pointing to the *Essay on the Government of the Colonies* of 1752 as an earlier expression of the theory of the colonies belonging to the empire only as fiefs of the Crown than is found in Bland's book of 1766 is somewhat tempered by opening a much earlier American work, *An Essay upon the Government of the English Plantations*, by an American, London, 1701, and finding this political doctrine there discussed by an anonymous Virginian author. This writer discusses also a Plan of Union of the colonies. Altogether the tract is an extraordinarily original production, not exceeded in interest as a political writing by anything known to me emanating from this country in the first half of the eighteenth century. Several students have sought to determine its authorship, but so far without success. One thinks at once of Robert Beverley, and then recalls the Hartwell-Blair-Chilton combination responsible for *The Present State of Virginia*, which though published in 1727 was composed in the period 1696–1698. There are numerous possibilities, but because Henry Hartwell was described in the *Present State of Virginia* as "bred in the offices" and a member of the Virginia Council, one may suggest him as especially likely to have possessed the knowledge and interest needed for the writing of such a book as the *Essay upon the Government of the English Plantations*. Its passage on a Plan of Union is printed and commented upon by Frederick D. Stone in his "Plans for the Union of the British Colonies of North America, 1643–1776," an admirable piece of research found in Hampton L. Carson's *History of the Celebration of the One Hundredth Anniversary of the Constitution of the United States*, 2 vols., Philadelphia, 1889, II, 439–503.

82. See Appendix I.

83. For title see Wroth, "James Sterling: Poet, Priest, and Prophet of Empire" in the *Proceedings of the American Antiquarian Society*, April, 1931, page 34. See also Sabin, Nos. 91331 and 91332.

84. Wroth, work cited in note above, pages 25–76. See also Sabin,

No. 91330, especially for the imprint and collation of a previously un-recorded Dublin edition of 1752.

85. William Smith, *The History of the Province of New-York*, page 136.

86. Franklin to Jared Eliot, Smyth, *Writings of Benjamin Franklin*, III, 280.

87. Sabin, No. 49695; Phillips, *Maps of America*, page 573. The results of an exhaustive study of this map by Colonel Lawrence Martin, chief of the Division of Maps, Library of Congress, is one day to ap-pear in monographic form. In the meantime an extensive abstract of this unpublished work is to appear in the forthcoming Vol. III, pages 328–351, of Hunter Miller's *Treaties and other International Acts of the United States*, where also, page 328, will be given a list of references to articles on the map published by Colonel Martin in various places in the period 1925 to 1933.

88. Dr. Mitchell's name occurs frequently as one of the principals in the correspondence of Colden, Franklin, and Bartram. The incident referred to is found in *Colden Papers*, IV, 287, 405–406.

89. Smyth, *Writings of Benjamin Franklin*, X, 93, Franklin to Jef-ferson, April 8, 1790. In the same work, V, 485, in his "Observations on the Report of the Lords of Trade on the Petition of Thomas Wal-pole, 1772" (see Ford, *Franklin Bibliography*, No. 311), Franklin re-fers to Mitchell's Map as having been published through the desire of the Lords of Trade "to ascertain the territory of the Six Nations." The question as to whether either the Jay copy of the Mitchell Map, now in the New York Historical Society, or the King George copy, now in the British Museum, were actually employed by the commissioners at the Treaty of Paris in 1782–83 is discussed by Colonel Lawrence Martin in Hunter Miller's work cited in note 87, above. The conclusions there stated on page 349 are, on the whole, negative as to the specific ques-tion, but there seems little doubt that both these copies were in official use in London or in Paris in close conection with the deliberations of the commissioners in Paris.

90. Huske, *The Present State of North-America*, page 27.

91. Smith, *The History of the Province of New-York*, page 136.

92. Sabin, No. 49693. Colonel Lawrence Martin, Chief of the Di-vision of Maps, Library of Congress, a student for many years of Mitchell's writings and map, has called my attention to a passage in *American Husbandry*, I, 286, in which the anonymous author says that the Mitchell map "was accompanied by a bulky pamphlet, written by

the Doctor, and entitled, *The Contest in America* . . ." This statement is somewhat loose as to the map and book having been brought out together, but its attribution of the book to Mitchell has been accepted by modern writers as probably correct.

93. *Monthly Review*, August, 1757, pages 172–175. For information as to the identity of this reviewer I am indebted to Mr. Benjamin C. Nangle of Yale University.

II

THE WESTERN EXPANSION

IN discussing the great map of North America made by
Dr. John Mitchell in 1755 under the authority of the
Lords of Trade, I emphasized the desire that men of the
time were experiencing for new, general maps which
should show the boundaries of the separate colonies and
clearly mark the limitations, from the English standpoint,
of the North American dominions of France and Spain. At
the same time, I suggested that it was something more
than the political need so well served by the Mitchell map
that underlay this desire for a visual representation of the
country. Economic forces and forces of deeper origin,
from which I would on no account separate the imponder-
able factors of vision, romance, and love of adventure,
were now moving American men to acquire knowledge of
those Alleghany and Ohio regions which represented then
and for them the mysterious West, the elusive and ever-
changing goal of human aspiration for countless centuries
in the life of the world. Once more and in this place it was
to be shown that the great events of human history are
naught but beats in the rhythm of man's westward passage.
And chief among the earlier printed documents underlying the great movement in this land were the maps and
geographical writings of the Pennsylvania surveyor, Lewis
Evans.

THE EVANS MAPS AND THE "GEOGRAPHICAL ESSAYS"

These generalizations are brought down to the specific
case by saying that merchants, adventurers, politicians, and
land-hungry individuals in the colonies of the mid-eight-

eenth century were feeling an increasing curiosity as to what lay beyond the Appalachian range. Land companies were forming and colonies were reëxamining and surveying their chartered boundaries. The maps that Lewis Evans made in 1749 and 1755 were concrete expressions of this fresh and potent spirit of restlessness. This well-remembered writer and cartographer seems to have been a native of Pennsylvania; he was certainly a long-time resident of that province, in which he exercised the profession of land surveyor. I have found nothing yet to substantiate the description of him as "a skilled surgeon"[1] by the editor of John Bartram's *Observations in his Travels from Pensilvania to Lake Ontario*, published in London in 1751.[2] It is not by chance that I have mentioned this fresh and simply written little book, of which more will be said in a later section, for in its pages Evans first appears significantly engaged upon the work by which he is remembered. The *Observations* is the narrative of a journey to the Six Nations at Onondaga made in 1743 by three of the most interesting men of colonial America—Conrad Weiser, ambassador to the Indians; John Bartram, naturalist; and Lewis Evans, map-maker and promoter of the American West. Through knowledge acquired on this and on similar journeys,[3] Evans was enabled to give the authenticity of personal observation to his maps of later years. He published in 1749 a *Map of Pensilvania, New-Jersey, New-York, and the Three Delaware Counties.* Based upon his own journeys, surveys, and observations, and upon information supplied him by Cadwallader Colden of New York and by other reliable persons of his own province and of New Jersey, this map possessed distinct importance for the colonies named in its title. After its publication certain forces around him joined themselves to his own geographical interests to push Evans forward to a new and greater endeavor. As the result of investigations of wider scope, he published in 1755 through Franklin & Hall an elaborate essay on the question of western expansion. Economy in the use of words permits us to speak of this work as the *Geographical Essays*, thus expressing in two words the sense of the sixty employed upon the title-page of the book. Evans's *Geographical Essays* was published in two editions in Philadelphia, and each of these was issued with an appropriate change in imprint in London in the same year. Its purpose was primarily to serve as an analysis of his *General Map of the Middle British Colonies in America*, published at the same time and sold either with or without the descriptive book.[4] It has the further distinction of being a careful description of the country to the west of the settlements, containing information of practical value to intending traders and settlers impossible to record upon a map. Its author urged, too, as others were doing in those years, the establishment of a colony on the western border that would find in prosperity its reward for serving as a barrier between the older settlements and the French and Indian encroachments. In these days we should describe such a colony as a "bumper," or even as a "shock-absorber." In the several current suggestions for the creation of barrier colonies, I have not found, by the way, many expressions of concern for the human material of which they were to be composed.

On June 26, 1750, Lewis Evans, already well known through the publication of his map of 1749, was chosen by the government of Pennsylvania, then keeping a wary eye upon Virginia and the Ohio Company, to go secretly to the west and spy out the new land of promise. He was instructed to make maps, to determine the latitudes of places and the position of intercolonial boundaries; to list fords, portages, passes, and navigable streams; to locate mineral deposits, to appraise soils, and in general to garner information of any features or factors of interest to a government that might soon be called upon to defend its territories against invasion by rival colonies or by land companies with royal charters, or that might wish on its own account to set about the business of expansion. All this Evans agreed to perform for 100 guineas and expenses, to be paid his heirs if he failed to return from a wilderness until then known only through the reports of Indian traders.[5] It was on September 11, less than three months after the time of Evans's engagement, that Christopher Gist received remarkably similar instructions from the Ohio Company for an exploration of much the same territory. Gist's report went into the archives of the Ohio Company, where it remained until its publication in Thomas Pownall's *Topographical Description* in 1776.[6] Evans had been instructed by the Council of Pennsylvania to reduce his "Minutes into one connected Description, and deliver the same to us."

One regrets having now to admit a belief that this "connected Description" was never submitted by Evans, and that, indeed, the thrilling western journey[7] thus planned was never carried out. Here is an anti-climax that our narrative could well do without, but it seems to me that the implications of the instructions received by Evans from the Pennsylvania authorities are of such significance in the history of the westward movement that reference to them may not be dispensed with in this place. The effect of the episode upon Evans, furthermore, seems to justify its place in the story. Though frustrated in his hopes and plans, he forgot neither the general purpose of the expedition proposed to him nor the specific aims outlined in his articles of instruction. Compiled slowly and only in part at first hand, his map and book of 1755, private ventures both, were an obvious fulfillment of those instructions, approaching in sense and in form as nearly as possible the "connected Description" demanded of him five years earlier by the Council of Pennsylvania.

Though Evans relied upon his own surveys, when these existed, in the compilation of his map, he was notably indebted for the information it gave to the surveys, narratives, and conjectures of others—of land operators, hunters, travelers on various missions, resident frontiersmen, and intelligent Indians. The account in the *Geographical Essays* of the collecting of his data for the map gives that book place as a document of considerable interest in the history of cartography. We learn from it that, confronted by the task of mapping a large unknown area, Evans had employed, in his method of acquiring data, the procedure followed by Marinus of Tyre and Claudius Ptolemy in the earliest days of map-making. The parallelism in methods in the development of an art, a science, or an industry, no matter what seas or what generations lie between, is one of the fascinating aspects of the story of man in his adaptation to environment; that is to say, of history. Evans's *Map of the Middle British Colonies* was engraved by James Turner of Philadelphia, and, upon its publication in the summer of 1755, commended itself immediately as a work of general usefulness, and of reliability in details. During the next half-century eighteen editions, revisions, copies, and derivatives, piratical and otherwise, were brought out by various English publishers of maps.[8]

Because of the praise by imitation of which it was the object, one might suppose that the Evans map and tract were gratefully accepted by all their author's world. This was far from being the case. Franklin thought well of it, and in 1772 in his reply to a report of the Lords of Trade on the Walpole grant, described Evans as "a gentleman of great American Knowledge."[9] The cartographer Hutchins praised him, and Governor Thomas Pownall, to whom the map was dedicated, held him and his work in lasting esteem,[10] recording in his *Topographical Description* of 1776 an impressive tale of its service in peace and in war, in land purchases from the Indians, in allotting new western lands, in campaigns, and in disputes over the boundaries of provinces. On the other hand, Evans made enemies by his admission of the French right to certain disputed areas; by the suggestion that Massachusetts was cherishing ideas of independence; by his affirmation of the superiority of the Potomac route to the Ohio over the Pennsylvania route; by his insistence upon the great importance of the Ohio Country to the British interest; and finally, by his warning against the designs of private and chartered land companies, made up principally of Pennsylvania, Virginia, and Maryland members. An anonymous writer took him severely to task on some of these points in two letters published in the *New York Mercury* some months after the appearance of his book and map.[11] Evans replied to the first of these very fully in his second publication, *Essays, Number II*, carrying home the counter attack by a direct assault upon Governor Shirley and the northern plan and conduct of the war. The author of the *Mercury* letters may very well have been William Livingston, notable for a later and more elaborate expression of their viewpoint, or he may have been William Smith, Jr., whose opinions on this matter were certainly diverse to those of Evans. The first of these seems to have been responsible for an even fiercer attack upon Evans soon to be mentioned,[12] and Smith appended a defamatory personal note to a passage of two solid pages in his *History of New York*, London, 1757, in which he strove to refute Evans's scrupulous view of French right to the territory northwest of the Lakes.[13] Knowing Livingston's habit of newspaper expression, however, one inclines towards him as the author of the *Mercury* letters.

Loveday was well pleased on the whole with Evans's performance, though he foresaw that the *Essays, Number II* was sure to give rise to recrimination. As a Sir William Johnson man he relished his author's criticism of Shirley, and, in common with a writer in the *Monthly Review,*[14] felt that he had presented his case on all points with "the appearance of much solidity of argument, as well as honesty of intention." Professing to doubt this "honesty of intention" the partisans of Shirley seem nevertheless to have felt that his arguments called for refutation. They made united attack not only upon Evans's facts and opinions, but as well upon his ability and personality.[15] Loveday thought William Smith's attack upon him in his *History of New York* unduly severe, and he felt incredulous when he read the assertion in the *Review of the Military Operations in North America*, London, 1757, that Thomas Pownall had secured the dedication to himself of Evans's map by the promise of a post in the New Jersey government, and that Pownall had personally taken a hand in the writing of *Essays, Number II.*[16] The *Review of the Military Operations*, which generally goes under the name of William Livingston, is sometimes attributed to William Smith, Jr., and is said by still other bibliographers, apparently on the basis of an earlier literary and political association, to have been a composite production of Livingston, William Smith, Jr., and John Morin Scott.[17] The author of the *Conduct of Major Gen. Shirley*, London, 1758, said to have been Shirley himself, took pains to reply specifically to Evans's charges against that general.

The facts composing the *Review of the Military Operations* are said to have been procured by the writer, or writers, from William Alexander, afterwards called Earl of Stirling, who was Shirley's aide and secretary, and who went to England in 1756 to assist in Shirley's defense, and to seek, vainly as it proved, the confirmation of his own title by Parliament. Investigation of the history of a book sometimes leads one into unexpected places. In the present instance, we follow, gladly enough, three New York gentlemen into an alcove in Vauxhall Gardens, that famous amusement ground of eighteenth-century London, and sit down with them to a bottle of wine. Listening to their conversation we shall hear William Alexander, Staats Morris, and George Harrison discussing a recent meeting between Mr. Alexander and John Pownall, Secretary to the Board of Trade and brother to Governor Thomas Pownall, at which Alexander in denying the authorship of the *Review* admitted willingly that the book had been written in New York by his "particular friend," and that he himself had brought the manuscript to London and put it into Dodsley's hands for publication. Defiantly the New Yorker had asserted further in his remarks to Pownall that he could prove true every allegation in its text against Thomas Pownall, whom, to the brother's embarrassment and perplexity, he described with partisan unfairness as "not fitt to be intrusted, . . . void even of common honesty, & capable of any thing."[18] The three Americans were pleased at the result of this interview, but that is not to say that all their countrymen regarded the *Review* with favor. From the bibliographer's standpoint, it is to be regretted that Mr. Alexander did not actually disclose the name of that "particular friend" in New York who wrote the book, but with other evidence pointing to William Livingston, it is not difficult to think of that phrase as covering the closer relationship of brother-in-law. The *Review of the Military Operations* was reprinted in Dublin in 1757, with Washington's journal of the Fort Necessity Campaign appended; in New Haven in 1758; and, strangely it seems, in New York, twelve years later, in 1770.[19] Loveday never learned the extent to which Evans had been influenced by Pownall. He felt, however, that the story of the bribe, based, said the author of the *Review,* upon a declaration of Evans "in his last illness to one of his most intimate friends; who concealed it till after his death,"[10] was worth, without further support, just nothing at all as evidence.

It was impossible for Loveday to appreciate the full importance of Evans's essays and map in the year of their appearance, though even then he felt a constructiveness in their intention and execution absent from most of the matter that came to him at this feverish time. But many years later, looking over his books and appraising them, he realized that Evans's work had been well up amongst the tracts of the period that might claim lasting influence. Its political implications aside, its war emergency value conceded and discounted as of ephemeral interest, it still stood out as the first practical, informative document printed in the interests of the great western expansion that in his later years had wonderfully affected the fortunes of the new nation.

SAMUEL HAZARD'S PLAN FOR A WESTERN COLONY

It is necessary to qualify this last statement somewhat so far as actual priority is concerned, for sometime in the year 1755, or even earlier, Samuel Hazard, a Philadelphia merchant, began making plans for the establishment of a colony in the western country. Such a colony had been proposed in the Plan of Union adopted at the Albany Congress of 1754, and Franklin asserts that Samuel Hazard's proposals were based upon a conversation with him and upon a paper of his composition, which he had allowed Hazard to read, elaborating the suggestion of the Albany Plan.[11] Whatever the early history of the Hazard scheme may have been, and in the story of the western land-development companies it is almost impossible to make with safety assertions regarding priority, it seems to be true that by the spring of 1755 its promoter had obtained the signatures of more than 3,500 intending settlers for a rigidly Protestant colony to be set up in the Ohio and Mississippi Valleys upon lands within the Charter bounds of Connecticut.[22] The project came to nothing in the end because of the death of Hazard in 1758 just as he was about to sail for England to apply for his grant. The details of the plan have been known to historians chiefly through a petition presented to the Connecticut legislature by its promoter's son, Ebenezer Hazard, in 1774.[23] The proposals came contemporaneously to Loveday's attention, however, in the form of two editions of a broadside entitled *Scheme for the Settlement of a New Colony to the Westward of Pennsylvania*. One of these, issued before May 8, 1755, contained in addition to the *Scheme* a petition to the Connecticut Assembly; the other, dated July 24, 1755, omitted this petition, already favorably acted upon, and carried in its place an address to the King. Loveday was somewhat disturbed by the smug Protestantism of the Hazard proposals, and though he recognized the relationship in men's thoughts between French encroachment, the Roman Catholic Church, the Jesuits, and the Indian menace, he felt somehow that Catholics would have been allowed no part in the Hazard colony even if that damning train of ideas had not existed. He preferred a colony proposed, as was that of Lewis Evans, upon a basis of "full Liberty of conscience." Hazard's *Scheme*, in its first printed edition, preceded in point of issue Evans's *Geographical Essays*, dated, and according to its author's statement, published on August 9th of the same year. The *Scheme* in its contemporary publications is of the greatest rarity. The editions of it here mentioned have not been described by bibliographers, nor, to the best of my knowledge, have they often been seen by historians.[24]

In spite of their preoccupation with the war and with local political troubles, Loveday and his fellow citizens of the middle colonies were aroused to a high pitch of interest in the schemes for western land development, whether they looked at those schemes as settlers, as speculators, or simply as patriots convinced that the barrier colonies proposed by the Ohio and Loyal Companies, by Kennedy, Franklin, Evans, Pownall, and by Samuel Hazard of Philadelphia were to prove the chief protection of the older settlements against French encroachment and Indian invasion.

RELIGION, EDUCATION, SCIENCE

In the midst of concern for his country in the years of the French and Indian War, James Loveday more than once found that the large problems of national destiny had been driven out of the national consciousness by the intrusion of certain fundamental questions of religion which refused to await a more seasonable period for discussion and settlement. The necessity of justifying the ways of God to man comes upon nations like the winds, recognizing neither times nor seasons. It was one of these visitations that the colonies were now undergoing. Whatever the degree of his indifference to the jarring of the sects, neither Loveday nor any other American in those years might escape some effect upon his consciousness of that up-welling of emotion we know as the Great Awakening, that quickening of the religious life begun by Jonathan Edwards in 1734, and continued and heightened by the progress of George Whitefield through the colonies at various times in the ensuing ten years. Among the flotsam left upon the shores when the flood subsided was much that could be salvaged for the spiritual life of the people, but mingled with it was found inevitably a deal of absolute wreckage in the form of disunion, exhaustion of men and churches, and uncomfortable doctrinal questions that the people of generations past had been content should remain beneath the waters of their peaceful moving stream. But now in this land, especially in New England, was to rage once more that ancient

"fierce dispute
Betwixt damnation and impassion'd clay,"

which seems periodically to engross the minds of men, which is with us now, indeed, crying for settlement, even though it no longer finds its most effective expression in the sermon and in the controversial tract of clerical origin. Worn down by the struggle, the churchman has turned his energies to social service; the novelist, the psychologist, and the sociologist have snatched his weapons, and, jostling one another, taken his place in the lists. But in the mid-eighteenth century the clergy led the onset and bore the brunt of the counter-charge. The number and continuous flow of their books, the very tone of their writings are evidence of the spiritual restlessness that possessed their people, for then, as always, books were written and printed only in response to public interest. Elsewhere in the colonies men watched, some with passion, all with sympathy, while the descendants of the Calvinist immigration "burned through" the yeas and nays of "our deep eternal theme." Harassed by a public enemy, uneasy before perplexing constitutional questions, stirred by new scientific discoveries and concepts, intent upon the necessity for pushing farther and still farther the country's frontiers, the men of this time yet found essential to their peace of mind the solution, or, at least, the effort towards solution, of problems bearing upon the soul's salvation. This concern with a question of vital emotional and intellectual character seems to us, looking back, to give profundity and to lend variety to their experience. It may be that it is this seeming confusion of ideas, this prodigality of interests which mark off the greater ages from the lesser, which distinguish the Renaissance, for example, from the century that follows it, or the last half of the eighteenth century in America from the first half of the nineteenth.

THE HALF-WAY COVENANT AND THE NEW DIVINITY

It is necessary to go back some generations in the life of the country to gain an understanding of the religious problems that confronted the New England contemporaries of Mr. Loveday. We find in the early Puritan practice in America a strictness in the matter of church membership (upon which was based also full citizenship) that seemed necessary and good to men newly released from persecution and intent upon building a compact state in the midst of the wilderness to which they had fled for shelter. By the terms of the Cambridge Platform of 1648,[15] only those were admitted into the membership of the churches who belonged among the "saints by calling," men who professed regeneration and were able to stand examination upon their grounds for believing themselves possessed of special grace. Events and tendencies of succeeding years so ameliorated this conception of church membership that in 1662 partial privileges of membership, including the right of baptism for their children but excluding access to the communion for themselves, were extended to baptized persons of decent life who professed belief in the Christian faith, those, in short, who "owned the covenant" even though they made no claim to the state of election through grace.[16] The terms of this compact, in later times called derisively the "Half-Way Covenant," became as the years went by still more lenient in practice through the growing liberalism of a people living healthy lives, free from persecution, in a land of material opportunity. Very slowly it came about in some places that even the privilege of the Communion was allowed to those who were members by virtue of the Half-Way Covenant. The old distinction in the membership seemed in a fair way of being forgotten. Soon after the year 1700, Solomon Stoddard, grandfather of Jonathan Edwards, was proclaiming the Lord's Supper as a means of regeneration rather than as a visible seal upon it, and, logically, inviting those who "owned the covenant" to participate in the sacred rite.[17] While this liberality in thought and practice was growing within the church, the insidious doctrines of Arminianism, especially the doctrine of the freedom of the will, had been seeping through the walls set about it by its Calvinistic founders. The courageous conception that salvation was attainable through repentance and moral determination towards good was so sane and spoke so clearly of a beneficent God that it affected perceptibly current teaching and belief. Shocking as these innovations were to many, they might in time have been generally accepted by the churches but for the sudden intrusion of the Great Awakening. The insistence of the leaders of that movement upon rebirth by conversion as the sole basis of church membership portended badly for the comfortable ways of the Half-Way Covenant and for the ennobling doctrine of individual free will. Against the false security of the Half-Way Covenant, which allowed men "to rest content with an imperfect and merely intellectual religious life," and against the beguiling doctrine of the freedom of the will, Calvinism, under the leadership of the most brilliant of its American votaries, now made a stand which became the point of departure for a new system of theology, the "New Divinity" or "New England Theology," which has been called the chief American contribution to Christian thought. In 1749 Jonathan Edwards attacked the Half-Way Covenant by the publication in Boston of his *Humble Inquiry concerning the Qualifications Requisite to a Compleat Standing and Full Communion in the Visible Christian Church.*[18] Five years later, this same writer brought his genius in

[61]

metaphysical speculation into play against the doctrine of the freedom of the will. His great treatise of Boston, 1754, *A careful and strict Enquiry into the modern prevailing Notions of that Freedom of Will which is supposed to be essential to Moral Agency*,[29] is a work as cogent as its title is long and precise. In the same city, in 1758, Edwards published his *Great Christian Doctrine of Original Sin Defended*.[30] For those of us who are gifted with only ordinary intelligence, the sure facts that emerge from these works are their author's mystical certainty of the sovereignty of God, his belief that morality was the end of the Christian life rather than a means of attaining it, and his insistence that men attained that Christian life only by God's working upon them through conversion. The statement of these doctrines by Edwards brought about a controversy that extended far beyond the period in which our interest lies.

Though apart geographically and temperamentally from the heat of the conflict, Loveday nevertheless felt its shock. The division of the New England Congregationalists into Old Light and New Light camps repeated itself before his eyes in the Old Side and New Side alignment in the Presbyterianism of Pennsylvania and New Jersey. He observed the schism in the Presbyterian Church in Philadelphia which resulted in 1746 in the establishment of New Jersey College, now Princeton University, for the education of a "New Side" ministry. Intellectually he was not greatly moved by Edwards's works, though with his sure feeling for the authentic, in whatever form it appeared, he realized that the treatise on the freedom of the will was an ageless book, one that would be remembered as long as the subject itself continued to move the theologian and the philosopher. But the truth is that its matter touched upon a weak spot in his mental range. Like many of us, he was incapable of following the close and impalpable threads of metaphysical argument. Unlike us, he could not turn for relief from his feeling of helplessness before it to that page in Boswell in which is recorded an argument arising from somebody's mention of the work of "Edwards of New England, on Grace." Bogged deep in the discussion, and by no means victorious in the argument, Dr. Johnson closed the matter for all time in the minds of easy-going men by the assertion that "All theory is against the freedom of the will; all experience for it." "I did not push the subject any farther," said Boswell.[31]

THE EMBATTLED CHURCHES

But the discussion was not so easily closed in New England. The old Calvinism stood embattled at New Haven under the leadership of Thomas Clap, whose parishioners at Enfield had been, it is said, "like boys let out of school" when their minister left them and carried his rigors to the presidency of Yale College. Fearing the influence upon the students of the unsound minister of New Haven First Church, of the local Church of England missionary, and of a dissenting minister of the place, the president and fellows of Yale determined in 1752 to create in the college a professorship in divinity, the incumbent of which was to conduct the Sunday services in chapel as well as to teach his subject throughout the week. In the following year this body asserted by carefully drawn resolutions the unqualified adherence of the president, fellows, and faculty of the College to the faith as defined in the Assembly Catechism and in the Saybrook abridgement of the Westminster Confession. The College required the attendance of all students upon Sunday chapel, conceding only that Church of England students might attend their own church upon such occasions as the sacrament was to be celebrated. One would say that this local situation was without general significance were it not that in its attitude the College was championing a strong group in the Congregational and Presbyterian churches of the whole country. Out of its resolutions of 1753 grew a pretty controversy. In 1754, President Clap explained and justified its stand in a book called the *Religious Constitution of Colleges, especially of Yale College.*[32] Dr. Benjamin Gale, of Killingworth, replied with his *Present State of the Colony of Connecticut Considered* and for several years the war went on with replies to replies and answers to answers, with "A Gentleman in the East," "A Friend in the West," and other thinly concealed participants bringing to the battle much passion and a great deal of curious learning in the fields of church polity and ecclesiastical and collegiate history.[33]

It was in the course of this controversy that there was published in New Haven in 1755 the first edition of President Clap's *Brief History and Vindication of the Doctrines received and established in the Churches of New England.*[34] In this work, republished in Boston in 1757, Thomas Clap stated firmly the tenets of the original New England Calvinism, tempered somewhat by the dispensations of the Half-Way Covenant. In it, also, he attacked what he regarded as the disintegrating theories of the New Lights and the Arminians. Thomas Clap hated many things and hated them rigorously, never realizing, perhaps that the basis of his hatred of the men, institutions, and doctrines he attacked was fear of their influence.[35] But that aside, his book was a challenge at once to the New Divinity and to the growing liberalism of the time. For years after its issuing there remained in Connecticut enough influential church members of Clap's way of thinking to cause that challenge to continue as a force in the life of New England.

Even though he was not able to foresee the end of the New England controversy, our Mr. Loveday in these days acquired a good notion of the lines upon which it was to be fought. In looking through a copy of Jonathan Mayhew's *Sermons*[36] of Boston, 1755, he saw that the young liberal of the celebrated Martha's Vineyard family was an out-and-out believer in free will, and that he was just a little more than squinting at what then was known as the Arian heresy, the denial of the consubstantiality of Christ with the Father which became with Samuel Clarke one of the tenets of the earlier Unitarianism. When he followed the progress of some of these ideas in later years in the writings of Chauncy and Webster of the liberal Harvard group, and found them still being opposed by the stricter New Light conception in the books of Joseph Bellamy, Peter Clark, and others of Yale teaching, Loveday realized that here, in this alignment between Eastern Massachusetts and Connecticut, between the influence of Harvard and Yale, was being fought something that in essence was a battle of cultures. Though in some of its aspects the issue seems hardly understandable to us today, yet we can feel that the force and passion of its underlying ideas gave it a nobility not possessed by the present-day contention between the two ancient institutions, fought out by football players, building contractors, and statisticians.

Chief among the supporters of the Edwards school, and one who, in carrying its ideas a little way beyond those of the founder, gave a broader and more substantial base for the erection of a system, was Joseph Bellamy of Bethlehem, Connecticut. His notable work of 1750, *True Religion Delineated*,[37] brought into focus the doctrines of the New Light Theology and advanced a more liberal view of the Atonement than the Old Calvinism permitted. He was a vigorous fighter against the Half-Way Covenant and against those who refused to accept the doctrine of original sin as handed down through St. Augustine and John Calvin. Once in the bleak seriousness of that controversy, Mr. Loveday thought he had caught in the wording of two contending titles something like a flash of humorous purpose. Samuel Webster issued in 1757 his *Winter Evening's Conversation upon the Doctrine of Original Sin . . . Wherein the Notion of our having sinned in Adam, and being on that Account only liable to eternal Damnation is proved to be unscriptural.*[38] This pleasantly named book was replied to by Peter Clark in his *Scripture Doctrine of Original Sin, stated in a Summer Morning's Conversation.*[39] There was not much in the lighter vein, however, in the texts of the two pamphlets. Joseph Bellamy added his weight to the forces against the liberal Mr. Webster by the publication, as part of a collection of *Sermons* of 1758, of the *Wisdom of God in the Permission of Sin.*[40] In the same year he published *A Letter to the Reverend Author of the Winter Evening Conversation on Original sin,*[41] announcing towards the conclusion of his book the forthcoming publication of Edwards's "Original Sin Defended." There was, of course, no reconciliation possible between holders of ideas so flatly opposed as those which found expression in the tracts that have been named, and the end of it all was that the theologians of Eastern Massachusetts and their partisans advanced by logical steps into increasingly liberal positions, while in the country parsonage of Joseph Bellamy of Connecticut some sixty ministers were trained in the next generation in the tenets of the Edwardean theology.

Long successfully maintained, in spite of its austerity, against rival systems of thought, the "New Divinity" came finally to be what it remains today—the theology of a scattered few. But while its struggle against the forces of deism, Arianism, Arminianism, and Old Calvinism was in progress, no man could have predicted the manner of its ultimate defeat. No man could then foresee that one day great numbers of the contenders on both sides would slowly retire from the field through the roads leading thence to Episcopalianism and Unitarianism, nor that the growing rationalism of man would in time so completely shift the emphasis of his thoughts that the issues themselves would cease to exist in the form of their eighteenth-century statement. None could predict that time when the deep New England spirit would flower in Ralph Waldo Emerson, philosophizing romantically upon man in nature, and in Henry Adams, musing upon the Virgin Mother of God with a rapture and understanding hardly attained by her natural devotees.

A NEW PURPOSE IN HIGHER EDUCATION

When the historian of higher education in America comes to the year 1755, he pauses for a freshening of effort, recognizing that his narrative is about to take a new direction. In that year were granted the Additional Charters[42] by means of which were firmly established King's College, known today as Columbia University, and the College of Philadelphia, now become the great school of learning in which I have at this moment the honor of speaking. The conditions underlying the establishment of these two institutions suggest to him the birth of a new intention in American higher education. The founders of Harvard, William and Mary, Yale, and Princeton had looked upon the college as the necessary background of a learned ministry. The new colleges announced their function to be the training of youth in the ways of good citizenship by giving them an education based upon a broad scheme of culture. The difference between the old and the new institutions lay more in the original intentions of their respective founders, however, than in the actual conduct of the colleges. The proportion of graduates of William and Mary designed for the ministry had not been large at any time, and although this proportion had always been very large at Harvard and Yale, yet in 1755 the purpose of the three earliest colleges was becoming more and more that of the general education of the youth of their communities. But the founders of all these colleges had emphasized in charters and in other foundation documents the primary purpose of them as training schools for the ministry, and in varying degrees this conception of the college function had affected the courses offered the student. The founders of the new colleges at New York and Philadelphia broke sharply from the medieval notion that the function of the college was the education of the cleric. They took for granted that the higher education was desirable for the man of secular interests and occupation and proposed courses of study that seemed more broadly based upon human necessity and upon the changing experience of the current world than those maintained by the older institutions.

THE COLLEGES OF PHILADELPHIA AND NEW YORK

It was not mere coincidence that brought about the establishment in the same year of two universities bearing the same ideal. The young William Smith, a Scotch tutor in a New York family, exchanged ideas with the elderly Samuel Johnson, first president of King's College, in the period immediately preceding the formation of the New York institution. Johnson wanted Smith to remain as one of his tutors, and when Smith decided to accept Franklin's invitation to become head of the Academy of Philadelphia, expressed disappointment and regret at the loss. Both Smith and Johnson had read Franklin's *Proposals Relating to the Education of Youth in Pensilvania*,[43] and both Franklin and Johnson knew and admired Smith's *General Idea of the College of Mirania*.[44] Johnson declined Franklin's invitation to become head of the Philadelphia institution, but afterwards was persuaded to take over the presidency of the college then forming in New York. Here was a close, if somewhat crisscross, connection between the three men most concerned in the foundation of the new schools, and one need not go beyond this fact in seeking explanation of the similarity in educational ideals of the two institutions with their Church of England trustees and Church of England clerical presidents.

In 1749, Franklin published anonymously in Philadelphia his *Proposals Relating to the Education of Youth in Pensilvania*. In this piece, the very image of his shrewd, balanced mind, he suggested the establishment in Philadelphia of an Academy in which, because of lack of time in the life of men to impart to students *"every Thing* that is useful, and *every Thing* that is ornamental," the effort might be made to teach them those "Things that are likely to be *most useful* and *most ornamental.*" The Academy was incorporated in 1753, and in 1755, by the terms of its *Additional Charter*, it took on collegiate rank. For a year before this its head had been the Rev. William Smith, who had come to the attention of the trustees through the publication in New York in 1753 of a book entitled *A General Idea of the College of Mirania*. I have read comments by modern writers faint in praise of this book, but it makes little difference what they think of it. Its matter was not intended for them but for those New Yorkers of 1753 interested in the new college project. And so we turn to Samuel Johnson's letters and find him praising the piece and its writer in a letter to the Archbishop of Canterbury. Doubtless he must have expressed himself in like terms to the Bishop of Oxford, for that prelate replied to him in terms of warmth in commendation of book and author.[45] And we find Franklin writing to the proud young author: "I know not when I have read a piece that has more affected me; so noble and just are the sentiments, so warm and animated the language."[46] Mr. Loveday found the civilized pages of William Smith as refreshing as anything he had lately read of the current English essayists, and he was much pleased when their author yielded to Franklin's urging and came to Philadelphia. In later years, despite periods of exile and popular disfavor, this young Scotchman who had dreamed in his *Mirania* of running a stream of living water through the hard-baked fields of current educational ideas attained a position in the esteem of his city second to none in the affairs of religion, education, and letters.

The establishment of the College of Philadelphia on a successful basis was accomplished by the Church of England clergyman, William Smith, working in harmony with Quaker, Presbyterian, and Anglican without the discord attendant upon religious jealousies. The College of New York was less fortunate in this respect. As soon as it had become apparent that the Church of England influence was to be dominant in its conduct, as it had been in originally projecting the idea of a college, the opponents of that church began a campaign designed to hinder the passage of the charter through the Assembly. Chief among those in the opposition was William Livingston, a member of the Presbyterian Church, who was also one of the Trustees of the College. In his *Independent Reflector*,[47] a periodical maintained for the publication of weekly essays on various subjects, he began and continued throughout the closing months of 1753 a protest against the dominance of the Church of England in the college. Letters on this subject from Livingston and others, notably William Smith, Jr., and John Morin Scott, were appearing almost at the same time in the *Occasional Reverberator*.[48] Finding that James Parker, the printer of the *Independent Reflector*, feared to continue the publication of the *Reflector* essays, William Livingston and his associates became early examples of the columnist in American journalism, and in 1754 and 1755 contributed a series of fifty-three articles

under the caption "The Watch Tower" to Hugh Gaine's
New York Mercury. Mr. James Alexander and Chief Justice William Smith, father of the historian of New York,
signed their names to a letter of protest which appeared in
The Querist,[49] a pamphlet of 1754 also attributed to Livingston. The state of mind of the people of New York in
this period is well indicated in the opening paragraph of
The Querist in which the author writes that he looks upon
"the affair of the college which at present ingrosses all
private conversation" as "the most important subject that
ever called for the public attention of this province."
Archibald Kennedy, a Scotch Presbyterian, and a governor
of the College, whose work as an intelligent publicist has
been discussed in my earlier lecture, published anonymously in 1755 a piece entitled *A Speech Said to have
been Delivered . . . Before the Close of the Late Sessions
by a Member Dissenting from the Church.*[50] Proclaiming
himself a dissenter, Mr. Kennedy displayed in this tract a
degree of tolerance that might well have served as an example to some of his irreconcilable associates. His little
book was in reality a plea for the healing of differences in
the face of the French and Indian menace. Nearly half of
it was taken up with practical suggestions of offense and defense, the familiar matter of his other tracts with, perhaps,
a stricter local application. This book, from the printing establishment of Hugh Gaine, seems to exist in only one
known copy. Bibliographers are familiar with its title only
through the medium of the newspaper notice of its publication. The most elaborate of the known tracts on behalf
of the college charter was Benjamin Nicoll's *Brief Vindication of the Proceedings of the Trustees Relating to the
College.*[51] There were of course other replies to the attacks
of the Livingston opposition, to the "Reflectors" as Johnson calls them, but they do not seem to have emerged
from the newspaper columns into the dignity of the pam-

phlet. But that the work of one of these defenders was effective we have the word of President Johnson who informed the Archbishop of Canterbury that young William Smith (later of Philadelphia) had "wrote several things with very good advantage,"[52] and later we learn from a letter of William Samuel Johnson to his father the possibility that if "Smith would throw out some of his wit against them [i.e. the Reflectors]," it might do more good than solid argument.[53] One would think that with so many important men and effective writers of the Province in opposition, the bill for the establishment of the college would have been lost or drastically altered, but that was not the case. The charter was granted, the Church of England continued to predominate in the membership of the board of trustees, and the Rev. Samuel Johnson, a Church of England clergyman converted from Congregationalism, was appointed president of the College.

During these years, Loveday found cause for reflection upon the vagaries of mankind. He contrasted the Presbyterian control of New Jersey College with the struggles of Presbyterian and Dutch Reformed against the Anglican control of the College of New York, and in 1754 he read the tract, previously mentioned, on *The Religious Constitution of Colleges, especially of Yale-College,* in which Thomas Clap, president of Yale, explained how just and right it was that the sole governing influence of the Connecticut college should be the established Congregationalism of the colony. Constitutionally distrustful of liberalism and obstinately convinced that much of it was based upon envy, hatred, malice, and all uncharitableness, he could not feel that there was anything especially heroic in the conduct of the New York Reflectors. He recalled always with particular distaste what he felt was the malice and absurdity apparent in Livingston's conduct when he sought to create prejudice against the New York Anglicans of 1755 by digging out and publishing with an introduction the *Narrative of a New and Unusual American Imprisonment*,[54] a story of the high hand as applied to Francis Makemie, a Presbyterian minister, in New York some half century before. He was none the less pleased that the Anglican control of the College of New York proved to be so light in its exercise as to be hardly perceptible, and when the tumult had died, he was able to look with satisfaction upon the new colleges of New York and Philadelphia, announcing curricula devised for the education of the average man along the broadest lines of culture known to the times, an ideal clung to today by the American university in the face of a modern tendency to regard it as the training school of the exceptional man.

SCIENCE FINDS ITS TONGUE[55]

In the year 1755 arose in New England one of those ancient conflicts between Religion and Science, or rather between current conceptions of religion and a new conception of the natural world, which have been a concomitant of the history of thought since the Middle Ages of our era. On November 18 of that year occurred an earthquake in New England and New York that caused considerable material damage, and stirred to uneasiness the minds and spirits of men accustomed to regard extraordinary natural phenomena as portentous warnings or as punishments meted his children by the Ruler of the Universe. In the months following the earthquake of 1755, some thirteen sermons and at least one poem were printed in which that unusual catastrophe was proclaimed as the action of an angry God. Among these, because of the prominence and authority of their authors, may be mentioned the *Divine Power and Anger displayed in Earthquakes*[56] of Mather Byles; *Earthquakes a Token of the Righteous Anger of God*,[57] by Charles Chauncy; and *Earthquakes the Works of God and Tokens of His just Displeasure* and the *Improvement of the Doctrine of Earthquakes*,[58] by Thomas Prince. In all these the state of belief in connection with the phenomenon discussed finds expression in the wording of their titles, but perhaps we should allow Mr. Byles to represent to us the current belief in the following words from his sermon already mentioned: "But we must not imagine from hence, that an earthquake, because it may be accounted for on Philosophical Principles, is a casual event, or that some chance has happened unto us. It is God at Work, tho' he works by the Intervention of second causes. Tho' it is no Miracle, it is the effect of Almighty Power." The amplification of this statement is found in the heading to the second part of Mr. Byles's sermon, which tells us that "An Earthquake is not only the effect of Almighty Power, but a Token of Divine Wrath." Reading discourses of this character and observing the place of their origin, Loveday felt that in them the Puritan conception of God as the relentless sovereign of man had attained its logical ultimate, but he received at about the same time another work from New England in which he found the Puritan spirit justified in so far as it stood for continuous inquiry and hard thinking about the relationship of God to man and to the universe. The *Lecture on Earthquakes*[59] of John Winthrop, Jr., a New Englander by birth, tradition, and education, was designed to allay the fear of extraordinary phenomena by the examination of their natural causes. The problem now was being approached from another angle; determination from authority and by metaphysics had given place in Winthrop's work to the experimental method of modern physical science. Winthrop left aside as no part of the concern of a scientist the First Cause, or God, whose inscrutable purposes he did not examine, devoting himself to the observation of the phenomenon itself and the discussion of its secondary or natural cause. In recording the undulatory motion of the earthquake, its duration, its direction, and the velocity of objects overthrown by its violence, he brought together isolated data from which conclusions concerning earthquakes in general might be drawn, thus applying the method that since Bacon has differentiated modern from ancient scientific reasoning. In natural history and in medicine, American scientists had been for a long time listing and recording data in the effort to determine general laws; in those fields the methods of modern science were recognized and accepted; the battle for inoculation had been fought and won through the influence of the Mathers, even though the morality of making ill in order to cure had been questioned by some of the clergy. But it was in this decade of 1750–1760 that the more awesome realms were to be invaded by the scientist, that earthquakes and comets were to be rationalized, and lightning to be explained as the concomitant of given sets of physical conditions. Winthrop's theory of earthquakes was not accepted at once and without reservation. Thomas Prince attacked not only his apparent rationalism, his ignoring of the First Cause, but suggested a theory different from Winthrop's as to the secondary cause, expressing the opinion that the phenomenon originated in electrical action in subterranean chambers, and seriously affirming that lightning rods might act to draw this uncontrollable force to the surface of the earth and cause the dreaded disturbance of land and sea.[60] Loveday felt that Prince as the champion of the older way of thinking had said the last word in its behalf. The next utterance on the subject of any consequence appeared in the anonymous *Essay on the Agitations of the Sea, . . . To which are added Some Thoughts on the Causes of Earthquakes*,[61] published in book form in Boston in 1761, having previously appeared in 1758 in "a crude copy" in the *New American Magazine*. Completely rationalistic, the anonymous Boston author of this little treatise does not mention the First Cause or a Token of Wrath, but proceeding upon the basis of geological indications in various parts of the world advances a theory of earthquakes sound enough to find acceptance with little amendment by the modern seismologist. In the meantime, in Boston in 1759, a work on comets entitled *Blazing Stars Messengers of God's Wrath*[61] had been countered by John Winthrop's *Two Lectures on Comets*.[63] Before this time had occurred the investigations of Newton, Keppler, and Halley. Winthrop, at least, had profited by their studies. It was his distinctive service that he made his contemporaries think in matters heretofore regarded in New England as closed to lay thought and speculation, and because everywhere and in all times changes in lay thought ultimately force changes in clerical thought and compel the removal of books and ideas from the Index of conservatism, this dynamic factor in Winthrop's teaching is his chief gift to the life of his times. It had come to Loveday's knowledge that when Winthrop was appointed to his chair at Harvard, the overseers of that College had opposed themselves to a demand that the young candidate be examined in the grounds of his religious belief.[64] Seeing now the manner in which Winthrop's teaching might and did enable man to integrate himself with the physical universe, if I may use that phrase of psychological slang, he saluted the action of the college authorities as a service of the first order to the country, even though he doubted whether they had conceived their decision as making much difference beyond the immediate vicinage of Charles River.

In another field of everyday concern New England thinkers were taking the lead for the comfort and well-being of man. The harsh soil of the North had forced her from the beginning to give closer attention to agricultural problems than was demanded in colonies possessing richer and more easily worked land. The old slavery to the idea of an avenging God found its expression in 1749 in a sermon on *Some temporal Advantages of Keeping Covenant with God*[65] in which Aaron Smith advocated prayer rather than irrigation and instanced rain during harvest as a token of divine anger. But farmers of all times had listened to this sort of thing on Sunday and, completely insensitive to its invitation to lie down effortless under the Divine Will, had gone doggedly and more or less cheerfully to their battle with the forces of Nature early Monday morning. The patience and courage of the New England husbandman under those conditions were rewarded when in 1748 Jared Eliot published the first edition of his *Essay upon Field Husbandry in New England.*[66] Reading in 1754 Part V of the *Continuation*[67] of this work, Loveday realized immediately the value of a treatise in which the accepted methods of European farming were rationalized and adapted to the soil, climate, and seasons of America. Eliot was a graduate of Yale, a physician, and an experimenter in the practical sciences. Living at Killingworth, Connecticut, he and his son-in-law, Benjamin Gale, formed a pair prolific in ideas in the fields of science, politics, and industry. Eliot wrote on farming and the making of iron from black sea sand; Gale wrote on medicine and public questions, and encouraged most effectively the experiments of his fellow townsman, Abel Buell, in the making of the first American printing type.

Much of the scientific investigation carried out in the Colonies found publication in the *Philosophical Transactions* of the Royal Society. That great organization numbered many eighteenth-century Americans among its members and showed the most hospitable spirit in the acceptance and publication of American contributions. The papers of American origin, especially in the early days, often were confined to the description of oddities, but as the years went by, there were found among them in increasing number studies based upon the observation of cases. The experimental method, still in its early stages in this country, was at least an accepted rule of procedure among amateurs and among those who devoted much of their time and derived something, at least, of their living from the practice of science.

The year 1755 lay in the middle of a group of years of the utmost significance in the history of science. It would be a peculiarly gratuitous task to relate in this place anything of those experiments in electricity which Franklin, Kinnersly, Syng, and Hopkinson carried on in Philadelphia in the late 1740's, and which were first given out through the publication in London in 1751 of Franklin's letters to Collinson under the title *Experiments and Observations on Electricity*.[68] After further investigations the books entitled *Supplemental Experiments* and *New Experiments* were brought out in 1753 and 1754 respectively. Loveday could never learn why the printing house of Franklin & Hall failed to bring out an edition of this epochal work, and thus lost for America the honor of an early publication of the discoveries of the Philadelphia group of physicists. The first separate American publication that Loveday saw on the subject of electricity was a Rhode Island broadside announcing a series of demonstrations by Ebenezer Kinnersly in the following terms: *Notice is hereby given . . . that at the Court House . . . is now to be exhibited . . . a Course of Experiments, on the newly-discovered electrical Fire*, dated "Newport, March 16, 1752."[69] Before this time, in 1751, Lewis Evans had been lecturing upon the electrical phenomena in New York,[70] and in the decade following, Kinnersly, Benjamin Bates, William Johnson,[71] and others are found in New York and New England proclaiming the entry of a new and unmeasured force into the affairs of men.

NOTES

1. See Appendix VI.

2. This interesting work is discussed at some length in Chapter III.

3. The long extract from Evans's journal of this expedition of 1743 (see Appendix, No. V of Pownall's *Topographical Description*, London, 1776) testifies to the importance of the journey in his later work.

4. See the description of the Evans maps and pamphlets in Appendix VI.

5. This document and a discussion of it are found in Appendix VI.

6. There must have been a certain amount of circulation of Gist's report in manuscript. In 1755, the author of the *State of the British and French Colonies* more than once shows his acquaintance with it; for example, on pages 110 and 113.

7. This point is discussed in Appendix VI.

8. These editions, issues, copies, and derivatives are admirably described and differentiated in Henry N. Stevens, *Lewis Evans*, 3d. ed. London, 1924.

9. Smyth, *Writings of Benjamin Franklin*, V, 485.

10. Thomas Pownall's appreciation of Evans is commented upon in Stevens's *Lewis Evans*, pages 13–14. His reliance upon Evans's work is clearly shown, and fully admitted by him, in his *Topographical Description* of London, 1776, which is, indeed, a fully revised and edited edition of the map of 1755 and the *Geographical Essays* of that year. Pownall's correspondence with Franklin in later years indicates his continued memory of his former American associate. He announced on page vi of his *Topographical Description* of 1776 that any profit from that work was to be given to Evans's daughter. See also Smyth, *Writings of Benjamin Franklin*, VIII, 330. This Amelia Evans was Mrs. Franklin's goddaughter.

11. These letters appeared in the *New York Mercury* for January 5 and February 2, 1756. They are dated respectively December 1, 1755, and January 26, 1756.

12. See the *Review of the Military Operations in North America*, pages 105–106, quoted in full in our Appendix VI. The authorship of the *Review* is discussed in Appendix VII.

13. For a discussion of this note see Appendix VI.

14. *Monthly Review*, September, 1756, page 312.

15. Governor Morris of Pennsylvania and various members of his family were among the close friends and admirers of Governor Shirley. Add to this able and influential Shirley-Morris group such partisans as William Livingston, William Alexander, Shirley's aide, and William Smith, Jr., all of New York, all powerful politically, and one becomes aware of the strength of the interests opposing the Pennsylvania map-maker.

16. See Appendix VI.

17. See Appendix VII.

18. See Appendix VII, for the whole of this Vauxhall Gardens passage between John Pownall and Lord Stirling.

19. See Appendix VII.

20. See Appendix VI for this statement in the passage there quoted from the *Review of the Military Operations.*

21. See Appendix VIII.

22. *American Archives,* 4th series, I, 863.

23. *Ibid.,* I, 861–867.

24. See Appendix VIII.

25. A *Platform of Church Discipline,* Cambridge, 1649. For a full collation see *Church Catalogue,* No. 491, where the first line of the imprint reads: "Printed by S G at Cambridge in New England." In the John Carter Brown Library copy and others this line reads "Printed at Cambridge by S G in New England." A list of dates and places of publication of later editions of the *Platform* is given in Dexter's "Collections" in his *Congregationalism as seen in its Literature,* No. 1507, and more fully in Sabin, Nos. 63331–63343.

26. See for general reference Williston Walker, *A History of the Congregational Churches in the United States,* New York, 1894, Volume III, The American Church History Series. A clear and satisfying account of the doctrines, polity, and controversies of the New England churches is found in Dexter, *Congregationalism as seen in its Literature:* Lecture VIII, Early New England Congregationalism, pages 411–464; Lecture IX, Later New England Congregationalism, pages 465–518. The form under which the terms of the Half-Way Covenant first was published in print is [Mitchell's] *Propositions concerning the Subject of Baptism and Consociation of Churches,* Cambridge, 1662 (see *Church Catalogue,* No. 577), reprinted in London the same year with "the Answer of the Dissenting Brethren." (See *Catalogue of the John Carter Brown Library,* III, 80–81.)

27. Dexter, *Congregationalism,* pages 475 and 483n.

28. Evans, No. 6312. A thorough bibliography of the writings of Jonathan Edwards is in preparation by James Thayer Gerould, Librarian of Princeton University.

29. Evans, No. 7187; see Sabin, No. 21930 for other editions.

30. Evans, No. 8188; see Sabin, No. 21942 for other editions.

31. Boswell, *Life of Johnson*, Oxford University Press, 1924, II, 220–221.

32. It is, perhaps, pure frivolity to remark that this tract as printed in New London by T. Green is undoubtedly the most villainously punctuated book in the history of typography. Its learned author most certainly did not see it in proof. In number and in lack of consequence, its commas stand, as in Timothy Dexter's famous book, as if scattered over the sheets by a pepper-caster. The only explanation of such profusion is that at the time of its printing one of the little Greens was learning to set type.

33. A list of the pamphlets issued in this controversy of six years' duration is found in the old John Carter Brown *Catalogue*, Part III, Nos. 1050–1053 and 1053n, where acknowledgement is made to J. Hammond Trumbull for the information. These titles are found also in Dr. Trumbull's *List of Books Printed in Connecticut* under the names of Thomas Clap, Thomas Darling, Benjamin Gale, John Graham, and Noah Hobart.

34. The titles of the two editions of this work, New Haven, 1755, and Boston, 1757, are entered in Evans, Nos. 7386 and 7873. The correct pagination of No. 7873, however, is: [ii], 40, [41].

35. Certain English writers were anathema to Clap and his school. Notable among these was John Taylor, whose *Scripture Doctrine of Original Sin* and *Scripture Doctrine of the Atonement* influenced the whole course of the religious history of the period. For comment upon the part played by these works in New England see Walker, *History of the Congregational Churches in the United States*.

36. Evans, No. 7488. A reprint of this collection of memorable sermons, copy in John Carter Brown Library, was brought out in London with the following imprint and pagination: "Boston Printed; London re-printed, for A. Millar in the Strand. M.DCC.LVI . . ." 8vo, pages viii, 1–392.

37. Evans, No. 6462.

38. Evans, Nos. 8060 and 8061.

39. Evans, No. 8103.

40. Evans, No. 8081. This sermon finds place in a collection en-

titled *Sermons upon the following Subjects, viz., The Divinity of Jesus Christ. The Millenium. The Wisdom of God, in the Permission of Sin.* Boston, 1758.

41. Evans, No. 8080.

42. Evans, Nos. 7515 and 7540.

43. Ford, *Franklin Bibliography*, No. 75. In 1927 the William L. Clements Library issued *Benjamin Franklin's Proposals for the Education of Youth in Pennsylvania*, Ann Arbor, 1927, a reprint of the *Proposals* of 1749 with an introduction by R[andolph] G[reenfield] A[dams]. It was reprinted again in 1931, in facsimile, as the first publication of the Rosenbach Fellowship in Bibliography.

44. Wilberforce Eames, Sabin, No. 84614, gives title, collation, and an interesting note.

45. H. & C. Schneider, *Samuel Johnson*, IV, 3–4 and II, 331–332. Of special interest in connection with this book is Smith's long letter to Johnson of [May, 1753]?, work cited above, I, 167–169.

46. Work cited in preceding note, I, 168, and Smyth, *Writings of Benjamin Franklin*, III, 131–133.

47. The whole subject of the character, influence, and authorship of the letters comprising the *Independent Reflector*, the *Occasional Reverberator*, and the *Watch Tower* is discussed fully and with evidence of the most intense scholarly industry in Richardson, *A History of Early American Magazines*, 1741–1789, pages 74–94. One of the chief services of Dr. Richardson's investigation of these publications is to apportion the responsibility for the various *Reflector* essays among Livingston, William Smith, Jr., and John Morin Scott. See also Wilberforce Eames in note to Sabin, No. 84576.

48. See preceding note.

49. Evans, No. 7228; Sabin, No. 67115. Partly reprinted in H. & C. Schneider, *Samuel Johnson*, IV, 208–212. See also the important note by Wilberforce Eames to Sabin, No. 84558, concerning this protest by James Alexander and Judge Smith.

50. For evidence of Kennedy's authorship of this tract see Appendix I.

51. Evans, No. 7282. Reprinted in H. & C. Schneider, *Samuel Johnson*, IV, 191–207. On December 8, 1754 (work cited, IV, 33), Samuel Johnson wrote to his sons, with his step-son, Benjamin Nicoll, in mind: "But I hope our Reflectors will be thoroughly mortified before the week is up by an excellent piece of your brother Benny's in defense of the trustees . . ." Nicoll's *Brief Vindication* was advertised as "just

published" in a supplement to the *New York Mercury* dated January 13, 1755.

52. H. & C. Schneider, *Samuel Johnson*, IV, 4.

53. *Ibid.*, IV, 31.

54. Evans, Nos. 1300 and 7455. Sedgewick, *Life of William Livingston*, page 110, writes in a note: "I have a receipt from Hugh Gaine, dated 28th Nov., 1755, for 15*l*, paid him as the proportion of Mr. Livingston and Mr. Alexander, for printing the trial of McKeemie and the Watch Tower." Proposals for the publication of Makemie's *Narrative* by subscription were published in the *New York Mercury* for March 31, 1755, when the editor announced the price would be raised to 2 shillings because he intended to prefix a dedication to the Assembly. It was announced in the same paper on April 7th that "Thursday next will be published" a *Narrative*, etc., and on April 14th, the book was advertised as "just published."

55. For most of the general ideas and specific examples cited in this section on science, I am indebted to the excellent doctor's thesis, as yet unpublished, *The Literature of Natural and Physical Science in the American Colonies to 1765*, by Winthrop Tilley, Ph.D., Brown University, 1933.

56. Evans, No. 7375 gives title and collation, which, however, should read: Pages [i–iv], 1–31.

57. Evans, No. 7380; [Paul Leicester Ford], *Bibliotheca Chaunciana*, No. 30.

58. Evans, Nos. 7549 and 7550. The first-named of these works had been published originally in 1727 on the occasion of the earthquake of October 29th of that year. See Evans, No. 2945.

59. Evans, No. 7597.

60. In the unpublished work cited in note 55, Mr. Tilley discusses in detail, and with full appreciation of its importance in the history of American ideas, this earthquake controversy between Winthrop and Prince.

61. Evans, No. 8851.

62. Evans, No. 8301.

63. Evans, No. 8522.

64. In the work cited in note 55, Mr. Tilley gives an excellent account of Winthrop's appointment to the Harvard chair.

65. Evans, No. 6418.

66. Evans, No. 6132 and, for a Boston reprint of the same year, No. 6133.

67. Evans, No. 7190 and, for a New York reprint of the same year, No. 7191.

68. See Ford, *Franklin Bibliography*, Nos. 77–82, 93–97.

69. *Rhode Island Imprints*, page 13, where is also recorded an advertisement of a similar lecture to be given by Benjamin Bates in Providence some weeks later.

70. Stokes, *Iconography of Manhattan Island*, IV, 628.

71. *A Course of Experiments . . . in . . . Electricity*. By William Johnson. New York, Hugh Gaine, 1764, seems to be unknown to bibliographers. A copy is in the John Carter Brown Library.

III

HISTORY AND LITERATURE

IN the account now to be given of certain works of history and literature found upon Mr. Loveday's shelf of 1755, there will be no mention of what we call the works of polite literature, of the carefully wrought essay or the studied ode characteristic of the period. This omission must not be taken as indicating a lack of appreciation of the part played by specimens of those and other types of belles lettres in the life of the time and place, and, therefore, of their importance in the general study of history and letters. Reflections, generally, of the neoclassical literature of eighteenth-century England, those writings possess, among critics and historians, champions in plenty who will continue to tell us of their meaning and value. They are in so little danger of being neglected that I feel free to ignore in this place the few that fall within our crowded decade, substituting for them another group of writings which were not literature in the intention of their authors, which lack, first of all, the imaginative quality usually associated with that term, but which, arising from conditions inherent in the life of the new land, seem to me to possess elemental importance in the American literary tradition. Composed of works of history, accounts of travel and captivity, Indian Treaties, and narrative poems, the books of this group seem to glow as from a fire within, to give forth a warm and living light rather than beams reflected from the polished surfaces of the eighteenth-century essay and ode. For reasons of chronology, I begin the discussion of these with a book that to some may glow but dimly, but which nevertheless has at its core an enduring fire.

Thomas Prince's *Chronological History of New England in the Form of Annals*,[1] of which the first volume was published in 1736, was brought again to the attention of readers when in 1754 its learned author began in Boston the publication in parts of a second volume with the changed title, *Annals of New England*.[2] The perusal of No. I of this new volume, issued in 1754, and of Nos. II and III of 1755, "all published," as the booksellers say, left Loveday thinking that in the long period of years between the conclusion of Volume I of the "New England Annals" and this beginning of Volume II, Mr. Prince had gained nothing in the art of arousing interest in his matter and had lost nothing of the ability to make an accurate and concise statement of facts. The book was deeply based upon love of the land and upon veneration for the strong and consecrated men of old who had given the New England community a special quality. About the time of its resumption, one of Mr. Loveday's schooners brought him a cask of special sherry which an appreciative neighbor described as a "rich, dry, and nutty" wine. Always in thinking of Prince's book, this phrase came back to Mr. Loveday. "Sound as a nut," he thought, "and as dry, but dry without aridity and rich without unctuousness."[3] He thought it a great pity when the book came to an end with the publication of No. III of the new volume. The cessation through lack of support of so important a garnering of verified fact (". . . I cite my vouchers to every passage . . ." wrote Prince), could only be regarded as a loss to American historiography by his own and later generations. The shade of Thomas Prince, a thoroughgoing book collector in his time, must today wander uneasily through the public and private libraries of his country, vexed that so few of them have ever been able to secure in original parts with covers intact all three numbers of his unfinished volume.

Rather liking "a bit of butter to his bread," if I may change the metaphor from terms of drink to terms of food, Mr. Loveday found himself compensated for the dry toast of integrity served him in Prince's *Chronological History* by the richer fare of William Douglass's *Summary, Historical and Political, of the British Settlements in North America*,[4] a copy of which came to his desk in 1755 in the London edition of that year. In this work, broader in scope than Prince's "New England Annals," less accurate than that book, badly arranged, verbose, combative in style and point of view, Mr. Loveday yet found a portrayal of his country of a kind that he had sought vainly in the earlier publications by English writers which covered the same ground. He experienced a philosophic delight, furthermore, in the self-portrait of the author presented in the composition—the picture of the competent Scotch physician of Boston, possessed by the idea of telling truly the whole story of the whole of his adopted country, and telling it with all the strength of intelligence and sincerity and all the weakness of an impatient and unreasonable personality. Reading its often fretful pages, he understood the vexation of the Rev. Samuel Johnson, president of King's College, who in the course of a single letter to Dr. Douglass, had to thank him for his skillful cure of Mrs. Johnson's chronic illness and to upbraid him for asserting in the *Summary* that the President himself had gone over to the Church of England from Congregationalism in order to make sure of a richer living.[5] And he understood also the impatience with which many of the Doctor's Boston contemporaries must have read in the *Summary* the recantation of his opposition to smallpox inoculation and the intimation that his attacks upon the great prophylactic measure had been stimulated by the fact that its chief supporters were the local clergy.

The eccentricities of Douglass himself have weighed

too heavily in modern evaluations of his book. Some writers of later days, judging the *Summary* hardly worth remembrance as historical record, have none the less given it special attention, expatiating upon it as one of our early American freaks of literature, a sort of buffoonery played upon Boston Common by a clown in a scholar's hood.[6] Such criticism goes wide of the mark. The thing that matters in judging a book of the past is not whether it satisfies the standards of our own time, but whether it pleased, and possessed significance for, the people for whom it was written, whether, in short, it fulfilled the purpose for which it was intended. Loveday, for example, found Dr. Douglass's *Summary* of a peculiar and distinctive interest. Together with many of his contemporaries he had been experiencing national growing-pains, had been realizing vaguely but persistently that, despite appearances, the country he was living in was something more than an unrelated group of colonies, each intent upon its individual concerns, each somewhat scornful of the people and the pretensions of the others. He wanted to know this group as a whole, the history of its component parts, their economic state and potentiality, their political condition, and their geographical features. Modern critics of the *Summary* have overlooked the fact that its author was the first to attempt this story from the viewpoint of a resident American, but his contemporaries were not unmindful of this and other features of the study he placed before them. In his *History of New York*, William Smith, Jr. spoke of Douglass as a sensible writer and discussed his views with respect even though he wrote further of him that he was "immethodical" and "often incorrect." The author of the long notice in the *Monthly Review* for October, 1755, began his appraisal of the *Summary* with an expression of irritation at its faults of construction, but, going on, soon found himself writing that it was "a fuller and more cir-

cumstantial account of North-America, than is any where
else to be met with. The author appears to be a man of
sound judgment, and extensive knowledge; he delivers his
sentiments of persons and things with a blunt freedom,
which is not always disagreeable; an air of integrity appears through the whole of his work." John Huske wrote
at some length of the book in his *Present State of North
America.* Because of the light that passage throws upon
contemporary opinion of American historiography, it
seems worth while to quote it here: "Every Person that
knows anything of North-America in general," wrote
Huske, "or of any one Province in particular, must be sen-
sible that the Histories or Works of Mather, Oldmixion,
Neal, Salmon, &c. who have chiefly copied each other, and
of all that have copied after them, relative to North
America, might almost as properly have called their
Works Histories of Prester John's, or the Hottentots
Country . . . as Histories of North America. . . . Even
Mather himself, said Oldmixon in his British Empire in
America, had eighty-seven Falshoods in fifty-six Pages.
In short, there is not one Work yet published to the
World in our Language that in any Degree deserves the
Title of a History of North America, but Smith's *History
of Virginia,* and Douglass's *Summary, Historical and Po-
litical, of the first Planting, progressive Improvements,
and present State of the British Settlements in North-
America, &c.* published a few Years ago at Boston in
New-England. And this last is only valuable for being the
best Collection of facts in general, for a future Historian,
that was ever made or published. For of all the crude indi-
gested works that were ever submitted to the Public, I believe this excels them therein. And with respect to Limits
between us and the French in general, and of Nova Scotia
in particular, he is very erroneous.'" The critical portion of
this comment upon the *Summary* had been anticipated, in-

deed, by its author, who wrote in a footnote that "it is as much as my leisure time does allow, to draw the plan, and lay in the materials, a good artificer may with ease erect the edifice."[8]

In addition to the defects in the *Summary* arising from the cross-grained personality, the necessarily limited knowledge, and the busy life of the author, is the fatal circumstance that its plan of publication was interrupted in 1752 by the outbreak of a smallpox epidemic in Boston, and that the book remains another example of a literary project in which the author's desire outran his power of achievement.[9] The historical narrative came abruptly to an end with the unfinished section on Virginia, and its author did not long survive this enforced termination of his work. It is likely that even had he lived he would not have resumed its composition, for he had already found that the continuance of the book was becoming more and more difficult as the scope of his researches extended further into regions of which he had little personal knowledge. His death in October, 1752, brought to an end whatever hope of resumption remained in the minds of his friends.[10]

Doubtless there were some among Douglass's neighbors, a people much given, as we have seen, to gloomy reflections, who saw the hand of God in the fact that a smallpox epidemic had brought to an end the literary work of one who had been the most effective opponent of inoculation against that recurrent disease. But we may be sure that to the rationalistic Douglass himself the outbreak of the illness implied nothing of the sort. He was grateful, indeed, for the opportunity it provided him to record a conciliatory expression on the subject of inoculation. In this eirenicon, which concludes the *Summary*, he accepted the general principle of inoculation, but insisted that in the beginning of its practice, and even at the time of writing, it was ignorantly and overenthusiastically applied, and on that account had resulted in needless suffering and loss of life. Whether under the best of circumstances for study and writing, Douglass, with his personal contrariness, would have made a great book of his *Summary* is a useless conjecture, as are most conjectures of the sort. But it is true that the busy Boston doctor left behind him a work that, uncompleted in matter and imperfect in its conception of the historian's task, is yet the first American history of the whole country and an intimate, sincere, and virile composition.

Another important work of history by an American writer came to Loveday's hands this year from London by way of Franklin & Hall's bookshop. Just as the disorder of Douglass had been a relief to him after the strictness of Prince, so the sanity, restraint, and impersonality of Cadwallader Colden took away the memory of Douglass's lack of measure and his failure in reticence. The *History of the Five Indian Nations* had its faraway origin in a pamphlet called *Papers Relating to the Indian Trade*,[11] which Colden edited and published in New York in 1724, though it is emphatically wrong to speak, as some writers persist in doing, of this collection of documents brought out in a local political issue as the first edition of Colden's *History*, an entirely different work first printed by William Bradford of New York in 1727.[12] In the second and very greatly enlarged edition of the *History*, of London, 1747, the *Papers* of 1724 appeared as one of the appendixes, their earliest association with the larger and more important work. The second edition of the *History* owed its existence largely to the urging of Peter Collinson, who undertook also to see to its publication through the London establishment of Thomas Osborne. After selling 300 copies of the book, Osborne lost confidence in its future and, acting hastily, as the event proved, sold the remainder sheets to another publisher. In 1750, the purchaser substituted a new title-page for the old and brought out an issue of the original sheets under the description of "second edition." In 1755 another edition, entirely reprinted in two volumes, described as the "third edition," was published in London as a timely and informative work upon an aspect of American affairs just then very much in the public mind. Osborne, the publisher, played throughout the part of a meddler with Colden's book. He changed the author's original dedication from Governor Burnet, whom it fitted, to General Oglethorpe, with whom it had nothing to do; made his title read "the Five Indian Nations of *Canada*" instead of "*New York*," thus throwing away the British claim to the Iroquois allegiance through the geographical location of the tribes; added a section on Pennsylvania Indian affairs which Colden had not written; and finally "remaindered" the book in unnecessary panic. Though Colden seems to have controlled his spirit throughout this transaction, yet one can imagine that his feelings towards his London publisher were not of the kindliest. He would have been well pleased, doubtless, had someone told him the conclusion of a young English hack writer's association with this same bookseller five years earlier. "Sir, he was impertinent to me, and I beat him," was Dr. Johnson's golden summary of that relationship.[13]

Colden's *History of the Five Indian Nations* was almost the only book in English that pretended to give anything beyond the most general information about the manners and customs, history, and organization of that confederacy of Indians whose least doings were of importance to every pioneer along the Appalachian range, to every merchant in the towns of the Middle Colonies, and to every member of a colonial assembly. The fact that Colden's book is derived in its anthropological section largely from French sources simply means that the writings of the French Jesuits, and of those other French writers who leaned upon their work, provided the only large body of observation from which, short of personal experience, knowledge of the Iroquois might be drawn. In one of his letters to Collinson, Colden expresses regret that his busy life, much of it spent in Indian business, had left him no time to learn the language of the Iroquois or to study their customs at first hand, and that therefore he was largely indebted to others for his ethnological data. But his papers and correspondence show that he was a close observer of them as far as his opportunities permitted, that their problems and the problems of the Colonies in connection with them were constantly in his mind, and above all, that he did not hold them in scorn and did not hate them. And when it is a question of their past and current relations with the Colonies, Colden's narrative is reliable, well documented, and authoritative.

When this book on the Indians of the Six Nations came from the press, the genius of the English had not yet turned towards anthropological studies.[14] But for all that there must have been few intelligent men of the time capable of uttering the incredible dictum of Moses Coit Tyler, who, more than a century later, wrote of Colden that it was "impossible for him to redeem his book from the curse of being a history of what deserves no history."[15] What insensitiveness, what lack of real perception of the period he was treating, what imprisonment of the imagination is in that sentence! It never occurred to serious men of Colden's time, always conscious of the Indian influence, to take that point of view, and to us, looking back, the criticism of his work is not of its subject, but of the fact that through limitations of temperament and opportunity he failed to make a truly great book of the material at his hand. Even this criticism did not present itself to his grateful contemporaries, and Loveday's disposition towards the book was that which Franklin expressed when he said, in a

[93]

letter to the author, that it was "a well wrote, entertaining & instructive Piece, and must be exceedingly useful to all those colonies who have anything to do with Indian Affairs."[16] John Huske wrote of the book more warmly. ". . . as to Histories of the Indians," he recorded in his *Present State of North America*, "there is not one published in our Language that deserves the Title, nor any Accounts of them, that I have seen, are worth reading, but that of Colden, which is justly called a History of the Five Nations, and is a masterly Performance."[17] William Smith, Jr., though not very friendly to Colden for political reasons, makes constant reference to his book throughout the *History of New York*. The anonymous author of the *State of the British and French Colonies in North America*, published in London in 1755, cites it frequently by chapter and verse for facts and for general ideas, and many of the effective lesser tracts of the period witness by their use of it the immense gap in current knowledge filled by this work of the New York politician, historian, and scientist.

One of the chief points of interest to readers of Colden's book, then as now, was its inclusion of many of the more important Indian Treaties, or minutes of conference between various Indian tribes and the colonists. In an article on the *Indian Treaty as Literature*,[18] written some years ago, I attempted to show that these reports of conferences were literature in the usual sense of the word and that they were a new literary form without prototype among writings of European origin. The Indian Captivity, though it stands out from other American productions because of distinctly marked characteristics, has behind it a whole library of captivity narratives in Old World writing —tales of capture by pirates, of slavery, and of enforced residence among Turks and Moors. The Indian Treaty on the other hand has no literary progenitor. It grew out of a specific set of conditions in North American life. Similar conditions had existed elsewhere at other times, but never before, I believe, had they given being to a distinct and important literary form.

In the course of the English colonial contact with the Indians many formal conferences were held of which the records either disappeared, or went immediately into the archives of the colonies concerned and there remained. But this is not what happened in every case. Records of many of the more important treaties of the seventeenth and eighteenth centuries found their way into print almost immediately after the conferences closed. The fifty printed Treaties listed in Henry F. De Puy's *Bibliography of the English Colonial Treaties with the American Indians* form a section of American literature of a native cast, set apart from the other types composing it by style and form, by the fresh quality of their interest, and by the urgency of their message to contemporary readers. It must be explained that the Treaties merit the name of literature, that they are, indeed, only of first-rate interest when they record the conferences of the Middle and Southern Colonies with the Indians of the Six Nations and their allied tribes. The New England Treaties are usually without other than local trade interest. The Indians with whom the New England governors dealt in the eighteenth century were for the most part a cowed and broken race. Though there are certain notable exceptions to the statement, the New England governors met them in conference only to tell them what to do and to tell them arrogantly. When on the other hand the governors of the Middle Colonies met the Iroquois, it was a meeting of chieftains, and the high and noble manners of the Indian on those ceremonial occasions compelled an equal grandeur of bearing from the white man. The Indians brought to these conferences political acumen, sardonic humor, and scorn, and though they knew their doom was upon them despite their temporary importance as the balance of power, they proposed, remembering their fathers, to undergo that doom in the high Roman manner. In the meantime as they were ritualists and orators the treaty conference was their grand opportunity. Here they gave free rein to their love of symbolism and their joy in words. In their speeches we find a style that is forthright in sentence structure, voluble, full of lovely, unstudied metaphor, rich in the primitive concepts of the forest, and savored with terse, satirically witty turns of speech—a style all its own that grew out of the soil, out of this soil and no other.

The ritual utterances and the addresses of the Indians in the treaty conferences were interpreted as they were spoken, and taken down in English by clerks of official appointment. And lest some one should object that their characteristic qualities of style were conferred upon them by the genius of the interpreters, it must be explained that for the most part these were not individuals of literary gifts. They were, on the contrary, white men of small education who had lived from youth among the Indians, or Indians who had lived among the colonists long enough to acquire their language. From north to south, over a period of a hundred years, through the mouths of Jesuit interpreters in Canada; Church of England missionaries and unlettered men and women in New York; Conrad Weiser, Andrew Montour, and other Indian agents in Pennsylvania; unknown and unrecorded persons in these places and the south, we find invariably in the records of the conferences the same spirited, unvexed flow of words, the same naïve but effective metaphor, and the same shrewd skill in forensic usage. These minutes have every appearance of being literal transcriptions of what was said by Indian and colonial, and though now and then a parenthetical clause is inserted to clarify a statement, never is there evidence that

an effort has been made to give it a literary flavor. In them
are often set down, briefly, the speeches accompanying the
symbolic burial of the dead, condolence for loss of rela-
tives in battle, healing of wounds, and wiping away of bit-
ter memories, and, set down very fully, the words of the
speeches when the immediate business of the conference
had begun.

It must have been a recognition of the intense literary
and dramatic interest of the Treaties that led Franklin
to print for the English market two hundred extra copies
of the Lancaster Treaty of 1744.[19] William Parks of Williamsburg issued an edition of this Treaty with an historical
introduction containing among much else of interest a general account of the Indian procedure in treaty conferences.[20] The matter of this introduction appeared again in
1747 in a London edition of the Treaty held at Philadelphia in 1742.[21] In 1754, there was published in London,
edited by Dr. William Smith of Philadelphia, a compilation of Indian pieces entitled *The Speech of a Creek Indian.*[22] Though the authentic and the artificial jostle each
other in this book, the editor expresses eloquently the interest and beauty of certain extracts it contains from
speeches found in the printed Treaties. A caption in the
Gentleman's Magazine for June, 1755,[23] reproducing
some speeches at the Albany Congress of 1754, says that
they "contain not only the Sense of the Indians on our
State of Affairs there, but some Strains of native eloquence
which might have done Honour to Tully or Demos-
thenes." A young tobacco factor in Maryland wrote in
1744 to a friend in the Isle of Man: "I have sent enclosed
a Treaty lately concluded with the Indians, which will
give you some insight into the Genius of those people we
brutishly call savages."[24] Speaking of one of the chieftains
at that conference, the secretary of the Maryland Commissioners wrote: "His action, when he spoke, was certainly

the most graceful, as well as bold, that any person ever saw; . . . he was complimented by the Governor, who said that he would have made a good figure in the forum of old Rome. And Mr. Commissioner Jennings declared that he had never seen so just an action in any of the most celebrated orators he had heard speak."[5] Cadwallader Colden wrote of the Indians in treaty conferences: "They have, it seems, a certain Urbanitas, or Atticism, in their Language, of which the common Ears are ever sensible, though only their great Speakers attain to it . . . Their Language abounds with Gutturals and strong Aspirations, these make it very sonorous and bold; and their Speeches abound with Metaphors, . . ."[6] There is evidence in plenty, indeed, that at the time of their publication the Treaties were regarded as something more than political documents by discriminating readers.

The ceremonies of the Six Nations in treaty with the white men were those immemorially used on their own ritual occasions. When, for example, one tribe came to condole with another for members lost in war, the stricken people received the visitors with a ceremony called "At the Wood's Edge."[7] "All through the conferences," I wrote in the earlier description of the Treaties lately referred to, "in letter and in spirit, runs an echo of this lovely ceremony of the forest children, a thing as sweet and simple as the dew on the grass at that edge of the woods, where the gracious words were spoken and the weary visitors led by the hand to food and rest and comforting fires." And so at the beginning of the Easton Treaty of 1758,[8] we hear Teedyuscung, the Delaware, addressing the colonial officials who had come a tiresome journey to the conference: ". . . I with this String [of wampum] wipe the Dust and Sweat off your Face, and clear your Eyes, and pick the Briars out of your Legs; and desire you will pull the Briars out of the Legs of the Indians that are come here, and anoint one of them with your healing Oil, and I will anoint the other." The metaphor on these occasions was redolent of the forest and forest life. Friendship was symbolized in the Indian speech as an ever-burning fire, a clear road, a strong chain, a strong silver chain, bright and rustless. Peace was a tree with widespread branches, giving shade and rest to weary men. "We heal your Wounds; we remove your Grief," say the Indian speakers. "We put fresh earth to the Roots of the Tree of Peace." We may say, I think, that the Treaty was literature to the men of the time, and to the sensitive among them it must have expressed something of the poetry of the land they lived in. To us today, its contemporary political significance forgot, it is the most distinctive literary product of the country. Anonymous, or rather, composite in authorship, it records the decline of one race and the rise of another in language of unique freshness and beauty, affording true material for the epic that is yet to be written.

The Indian Treaty showed the native American to the Colonists in his nobler moments, recorded his racial loyalty, his shrewd diplomacy, his sardonic humor, his skill in postponing the tragic doom that he foresaw, and his rich and effective oratory. The other side of his character, his ferocity in war, his callousness, his squalid manner of living, and his greed, more apparent because of his lack of the concealing veneer of civilized custom, were made even more familiar than his finer qualities by the printed and often reprinted narratives of prisoners that we know as the Indian Captivities.[9] In many cases, these were the narratives of plain, unlettered folk; in others, of persons of education, even of learned ministers. Usually they were marked by the piety of their expressions if not by the Christian charity of their sentiments. All begin with the description of the capture, describe the shock of the event, the cruel march to Canada for ransom, or into the interior for the less enviable fate of adoption into the tribe. They dwell with horror, sometimes with horrid gusto, upon the torture of associates, or upon the brutal killing of men and women incapable of sustaining the rigors of the march. But often when the initial horrors of their state had been forgot, the captives found themselves slipping comfortably into the life and interests of the forest people. Sometimes they came back to their homes with a shamefaced praise for the domestic virtues of the Indians, for the lack of complexity in their rude Arcadian existence. Out of their narratives, therefore, along with hatred and fear and venom came to every reader a clear and broadening conception of another way of life, of an arrested but definite civilization close to his own in space yet separated from it by centuries of progress in the mechanical arts of living. The fascination of these narratives for learned and lewd alike seems to be attested by the number of editions they ran through. Loveday read in an edition of Philadelphia, 1754, Samuel Bownas's story of the captivity of Elizabeth Hanson, *God's Mercy surmounting Man's Cruelty*.[30] This was only the second of the six eighteenth-century editions of America and England in which it found publication. He was more immediately interested when in 1758 an acquaintance of his, a Pennsylvania trader, Robert Eastburn, returned from a short but eventful captivity in Canada and released his overcharged feelings in a *Faithful Narrative of the many Dangers and Sufferings of Robert Eastburn*.[31] That book set Loveday to counting some of the works of similar character on his shelf. He found there, published in the preceding ten years, seven editions of six different captivities. These figures made him realize to what an extent his reading had been taken up with Indian matters in his time. With an Indian Treaty on an average of every nine months and an Indian Captivity published nearly every year, with Colden's *History*, with the tracts of Archibald Kennedy and of numerous other writers in which the political aspect of the Indian had prominent part, it occurred to him that the dominating figure in the writing of his time and place was the American Indian.

To take from Mr. Loveday's shelf at this juncture a work by John Bartram, the Quaker naturalist of Philadelphia, is to open a window that looks down a new and pleasant avenue. The *Observations by Mr. John Bartram in his Travels from Pensilvania to Lake Ontario*,[32] published in London in 1751, is the record of an expedition undertaken by the famous botanist in 1743 in search of strange plants for his own Botanical Garden at Philadelphia and for the parks and gardens of a group of English nobility and gentry who for three years past had been purchasing from him seeds, cuttings, roots, and saplings of American origin. Disappointed in an expectation of making the journey in 1742, Bartram seized the "lucky opportunity" that presented itself when, a year later, Conrad Weiser, the Pennsylvania interpreter and go-between with the Indians, was ordered to the country of the Six Nations to bring about a peace between the Iroquois and the government of Virginia. Weiser received his orders from the Pennsylvania Council on June 18, 1743. On June 26, Bartram wrote joyfully to Cadwallader Colden: "I have lately received orders from London to travel, to gather the seeds of the Balm of Gilead, and other species of evergreens. The Duke of Norfolk hath subscribed twenty guineas, the Duke of Richmond and two other gentlemen fifteen more; besides our proprietor hath sent me orders to procure some curiosities for him. I am now providing for a journey up Susquehanna, with our interpreter. . . . We are to set out in a week or two."

When Bartram finally left Philadelphia on July 3 to join Weiser at his home in the Tulpehocken Valley, he was accompanied by Lewis Evans, the Pennsylvania surveyor of whom we have already spoken at length in our discussion of the Westward Expansion. It does not clearly appear how or why Evans was joined to the expedition, but we know enough of him to suggest that his personal inclination towards that sort of adventure would have been reason in plenty if others had been lacking. But whatever the train and nature of the circumstances that brought together these three men with their varied interests, striking personalities, and uncommon abilities, the journey they now made in conjunction turned out to be an effective force in American history, cartography, and literature. Out of it came, in order of mention: peace between Virginia and the Iroquois;[33] the memorable Lancaster treaty of 1744 between the Six Nations and the governments of Pennsylvania, Virginia, and Maryland; the record of that conference in the form of two editions of a notable printed Treaty; Bartram's *Observations* of 1751; and finally, as we learn from what is left us of Lewis Evans's journal of the expedition, much data that went into his maps of 1749 and 1755, and into his *Geographical Essays* of the later year.[34] Of most of these books and maps we have already spoken; we are concerned now only with Bartram's straightforward record of his journey to Ontario and return.

Although Peter Collinson, Bartram's friend and patron in England, wrote him soon after the conclusion of the expedition that he longed to see his journal, the perversity of things put off the gratification of his wish for a full seven years. Twice in that period the journal was sent abroad but each time the ship that carried it was captured by the French. It was not until June, 1750, as we learn from the introduction to the printed work, that it reached England in safety.[35] The editor of the book records that so many gentlemen had desired to see the journal of an expedition into a country then beginning to occupy the thoughts of Englishmen that its publication seemed the only way of gratifying them. Accordingly the little book was brought out in 1751 with an addition in the form of "An Account of the Cataracts at Niagara" by Peter Kalm, a Swedish naturalist who had associated much with Bartram in America.[36] It is an ironical fact that the chief interest seen in Bartram's *Observations* by the writer of its Preface was its political implications.[37] Nothing had been further from Bartram's intention than to enter the field of politics, but it is none the less true that his record of a naturalist's journey through the American hinterland was seized upon as an agency to direct men's eyes towards the great territory that the English seemed just then in danger of letting go to the French by default of action.

It is doubtful, however, whether the politicians found much to interest them in Bartram's simple narrative, and it is certain that the scientific men were disappointed in it. Peter Kalm expressed his regret at its publication immediately, and in later years wrote that it would not "be doing justice to Mr. Bartram's merit, if it were to be judged of by this performance."[38] But to us who look at it neither as politicians nor as scientists, these strictures mean little. We go to it for the delight of reading a plain but sensitive man's narrative of travel in a new and lovely land. For the sake of Bartram's reputation among his contemporaries we might wish that he had crammed his journal with the great knowledge Kalm claimed for him, but for our own satisfaction we are content that he left it as it is.

Bartram's *Observations* is a slender book in size, and some may agree with Kalm that it is slight in content, but to our Mr. Loveday, wearied of the political and religious controversy of the period, it must have seemed, as it does to many today, an extraordinarily refreshing composition in style and matter. In it we find the day-by-day record of one whose only concern was to see and to feel to the full extent of a sensitive, enthusiastic, and tolerant nature—a man without learning save in things of field and forest, of no preoccupation with politics or religion, devoid of hatreds and rivalries, a partisan of no cause but the cause of the trees and the plants and the animals. In the easy, straightforward style of expression often vouchsafed men of action, he set down the detail of his journey, pictured the face of the country, described the food, manners, and amusements of the Indians he encountered, and recorded the actual measurements of the communal dwellings from which the Indians of the Long House took their name. Our Mr. Loveday felt in the book a delightful quality of innocence. It spoke to him of noble hardwood forests, of sunny glades and wind-swept uplands, of swift rivers and teeming swamps. As fresh and kind as Spring, as pagan as the forests and as Christian as the sweet and simple nature of its writer, it must have brought a brief release to many then greatly taken up with grave matters of public and private conscience. Loveday experienced one regret concerning it that we, too, must feel. What a book it would have made, he thought, if Conrad Weiser's journal of his conference with the Indians at Onondaga and Evans's journal of the expedition had been added to Bartram's account of the journey there and back! But Evans's record has never been published in full, and Weiser's journal, unfortunately, was published only in the nineteenth century. We know today that the first of these, rich in topographical observation, was likewise charged with prophecy, and we know that the second embodied a full record of one of the finest of the Indian Treaties, the record of a conference held at the capital and chief Council Fire of the Six Nations in the very heart of the great forest.

Earlier in this examination we spoke of the heroic quality of the *Journal* of Christian Frederick Post which

Franklin, with his sure recognition of excellence, appended to the *Enquiry* of Charles Thomson when he brought out that book in London in 1759.[39] In that same year Post's *Second Journal*[40] also was published in London in separate form, apparently at Franklin's expense. The two together form a record of experience that should be better known to all of us. The journals of Post make up their lack of such charm as is found in Bartram's *Observations* by the possession of extraordinary dramatic interest, of the sense of urgency and of great matters impending. The defeat of Braddock had given the French opportunity to seek and attain the allegiance of the western Indians—those tribes of the Ohio country normally under control of the Six Nations and therefore friendly in theory to the English. The new alliance of these tribes with the French was the great barrier in the way of the recapture of Fort Duquesne by the British forces. Advised and urged by Teedyuscung, the leading chieftain of the Delawares, the Pennsylvania government determined to send an embassy to the Ohio Indians in the hope of breaking the new alliance, and because of his known courage, zeal, and love of man, Christian Frederick Post, the Moravian missionary, was chosen for that difficult and perilous service. On July 15, 1758, Post set out for the Ohio.[41] In danger from the French and their Indian allies every step of the way, alone but for three Indian guides (one of them a deserter in a time of special peril, and another a daily menace because of an evil and unstable temper), Post spent the next two months in travel and in negotiation with the disaffected Indians. Under the guns of French forts, in the very presence, often, of French officers, he harangued and pleaded with the savages to renounce their unwise and unnatural allegiance to the ancient foe. In his speeches and debates on these occasions he betrayed all the shrewdness of an eighteenth-century politician, all the boldness and simplicity of a primitive Christian. Not only was it a matter, throughout, of touch and go as far as his own life was concerned, but the success of his mission was in doubt until, at the very end of his second visit to the west, he had the satisfaction of obtaining a promise of neutrality from the Indians. As the result of that agreement, General Forbes was unhindered in his progress to Duquesne, and the western phase of the war was brought to an end. Loveday first read Post's journals as the record of an action of extraordinary importance in a crisis of public affairs; he came back to them more than once in later years as exciting and authentic narratives of high adventure.

Before leaving Mr. Post in that dangerous wilderness, I must show you that he was not entirely without protection. In doing this I shall be able to gratify myself by quoting one of those Indian speeches that always seem to me to have a quality of saltiness seldom found in the English writing of that period or of ours. This particular speech is an example also of the high courtesy of the Indian in his formal moments, of his metaphorical language, and of a certain subtlety in the paying of a compliment that was a feature of their manners. At the conclusion of Post's first journey, the chieftains, King Beaver and Shingas, turned to Pisquetomen, who had guided Post to them, and charged him in these words: "Brother, you told us, that the Governor of Philadelphia and Teedyuscung took this Man out of their Bosoms and put him into your Bosom, that you should bring him here; and you have brought him here to us, and we have seen and heard him, and now we give him into your Bosom to bring him to the same Place again before the Governor; but don't let him quite loose; we shall rejoice when we shall see him here again."

Another personal narrative that lies in some category between the patriotic poem and the Indian Captivity was the *Gallic Perfidy* of John Maylem.[42] This young Rhode

Islander, an ensign in the New England forces that helped garrison Fort William Henry, was among those who escaped the hatchet and knife when Montcalm's Indians got out of hand and massacred the colonials as they left the surrendered wilderness fort. War was meat and drink to John Maylem. He began singing it before he was old enough to carry a gun. His first poem, *The Conquest of Beausejour*,[43] was written in 1755 at the age of sixteen. His second, *Gallic Perfidy*, a narrative of personal experience, was published in 1758 under the pseudonym "Philo-Bellum." In it he told the story of his capture at Fort William Henry, the long journey to Montreal, his detention there, and his subsequent ransom. The heroic measure he adopted for the poem gave opportunity for the expression in lofty terms of his rage and his hatred of the French, and allowed him to call stirringly for vengeance upon what he and many others chose to believe was Montcalm's perfidy. It is not great poetry, but it is competent verse, embodying qualities of passion, distress, and fear, fit matter for the reading of men whose emotions were at the pitch. Maylem's personal desire for revenge was partially satisfied when some months later he took part in the capture of Louisburg. His long poem, *The Conquest of Louisbourg*,[44] Boston, 1758, is in the epic style, and lacking the bitterness of defeat, it lacks also the vivid and more obvious human feeling of *Gallic Perfidy*. Loveday found these poems moving as well as readable, but not so moving as he could have wished. He thought it would have been a fine thing if his country had produced in this crisis a poet of really great parts, but he felt that Maylem's ambitious efforts were not sufficiently memorable in expression to overcome the narrowness of interest that normally confines the topical and episodic within the bounds of a period. These narratives in verse, therefore, do not take a high place in our poetic heritage, though they are truly enough part of our racial memory. Conceived as literature by their author, they remain today as documents, rather more impassioned than most, to vivify the history of his period.

CONCLUSION

IN beginning this examination of American writing of the years just before and just after 1755, I suggested that though I had no thesis to establish, I was not without a purpose in choosing the subject and the method of treatment then outlined. Briefly that purpose was to determine whether familiarity with the books that came currently to the desk of an educated American of the period might not give us a clearer understanding of our forefathers and of the ideas that occupied them.

In order to carry out the examination then proposed we have gone through a selection of books which, it seemed, might easily have been known to a representative man of affairs of that time. In the course of this investigation of Mr. Loveday's reading, we have found that he was compelled to devote himself to the consideration of a perplexing variety of subjects. In the field of colonial politics he was concerned with the obvious French encroachment upon the boundaries of the Colonies. In order to understand clearly his country's contention in the matter of territorial rights he was compelled to review the whole course of British and French relations since the two empires had first come into contact in North America, and, as a consequence of that review, to refresh himself in the general history of Europe in the century preceding his own.

Because a part of the scheme of defense against the French was the formation of a union of the British colonies, Loveday found himself at this time pondering the difficulties in the way of federation and the obvious advantages of such a policy. This particular constitutional problem was never again to be absent from his mind until the final union of the colonies came about under the Federal

Constitution some forty years later. Associated with this question were the contrasting theories of the relationship of the Colonies to the crown and realm of England, a question that seemed faintly academic at that time but which became actual and imperative when Parliament in the next decade brought it abruptly forward by the imposition of the stamp taxation. In his own colony, and in several others, the bickering between assemblies and royal or proprietary governors was raising still different questions of constitutional import in which personal and local animosities often confused the essential issue, the status, that is, in law and in fact, of the colonized English subject. Running alongside these problems, so soon to become issues, was the question of the Indian—the matter of retaining his affiliation in war and the even more perplexing decision to be made as to the manner in which his rights to the land and the white man's hunger for it were to be reconciled in the light of human justice and decency. And as if these were not enough questions to keep him occupied, his aggressive countrymen demanded his attention in the midst of everything by their plans for settling the territory at that moment the object of contention between themselves and the French, themselves and the Indian, the French and the Indian, and between one British colony and another. The several public problems before him seemed to overlap and to pile one upon another in a manner the most confused, but perhaps a condition does not really present a problem unless it is so wrapped up in other conditions that right, wrong, and expediency seem hopelessly intermingled. Or so it seemed to Mr. Loveday in those years of war and political confusion in which, unwittingly, he was being instructed for the greater events of the next generation.

In those years, too, Mr. Loveday's countrymen felt themselves compelled to bring up old questions of religious faith and doctrine, to dispute with bitterness and passion the problems of church membership, freedom of the will, and election by grace or conversion. He saw old barriers strengthened in one place and weakened in another; heard of consolidations and of schisms; heard the thunderous assertions of fundamentalism and the whispered question of a new-born rationalism that in the end compelled the whole battle line to change its front. It was an exhibition of the unaccountable resiliency of the human spirit that with all these questions of war, politics, and religion demanding answers, two great communities, New York and Philadelphia, set themselves to consider the problems of training their youth in the higher learning, and succeeded in establishing colleges that marked the beginning of a new tradition in American education. And it was now that the ground was laid for the progress in electrical discovery that brought in a new world of science and industry, and now that men of learning sought to remove from such natural phenomena as earthquakes, comets, and tidal waves the conception of punishment by an angry and vindictive God so long associated with them in human belief.

It was probably the critical conditions of these years that set men to the study of the country itself; that stirred Mr. Prince to the resumption of the "New England Annals" so long in abeyance; that gave impetus to Dr. Douglass's efforts to relate satisfactorily the story of the whole group of British American colonies; that urged Cadwallader Colden to rewrite and revise his account of the Iroquois Confederacy. It was certainly the unsettled political condition that brought into print in this period so many Indian Treaties; that caused the Indian in a score of books and tracts to assume a part of consequence in the thoughts of the people; that put the Indian and the frontier so prominently into their writing as to mark its chief divergence from older literatures.

Because the spirit of imagination left so small a record of its presence in the writings of this period, our inquiry is perforce limited to the social questions that occupied the mind of the colonial American of 1755. If he had given us a romance; if he had left for us one remembered song; if he had poured out his heart in a single unforgettable prayer or meditation; if he had oftener shouted defiance at the scheme of things, and if these expressions of his individual soul had found their way into print, we should have known the man himself more intimately than we have actually learned to know him from the objective writings we found upon Mr. Loveday's shelf. But it may be that even if he had left for us these legible indications of his inward and spiritual state, the shape of our examination would hardly have been altered. The existing books and pamphlets record, indeed, a varied life of the mind and the emotions, a life impressive for the breadth and dignity of its interests. They form truly a literature of expression, even if it is not the expression of the individual personality that we study with avidity today. They are marked by vigor, honesty, and effectiveness of statement, and in one notable case, that of the Indian Treaty, by complete originality of form. Seen and read as a whole, they portray an image of the times in which figures are seen more nearly in the round and with a greater depth of background than in the flatly painted picture which to most of us represents the colonial scene.

NOTES

1. Sabin, Nos. 65585–65586.

2. *Ibid.*, where the date of resumption of Prince's work with Volume II, Number I, is improperly given as 1755. Evans, No. 7301, correctly attributes Volume II, Number I to 1754, for the *Boston Weekly News Letter* has it advertised as "This Day Published" in its issue of May 30, 1754. It is not impossible that Number II also was published late in 1754, but I have not been able to find a record of its publication in any Boston newspaper. Number III of this volume contains on one of its covers (see S. G. Drake's reprint of the *Chronological History*, Boston, 1852, page 438) an appeal for data signed by Prince and dated May 28, 1755.

3. This wine with its contradictory attributes of richness and dryness must have been the ancestor of that "Pale Rich" sherry that Professor Saintsbury describes in his *Notes on a Cellar Book*, page 19.

4. See Appendix IX.

5. H. & C. Schneider, *Samuel Johnson*, I, 156–158.

6. Moses Coit Tyler's account of Douglass and his book in the *History of American Literature*, II, 151–157, would, I am sure, have astonished Douglass's contemporaries, who thought of his book as a serious and important history.

7. Huske, *The Present State of North America*, pages 41–42.

8. Edition of Boston, 1749–51, II, 392n.

9. On the page cited in the preceding note, Douglass explains the interruption by the statement: "The Printer and his People in fear of the Small-Pox, left their printing Office in Boston, and retired into the Country."

10. The death of Dr. Douglass is recorded on the inside front cover of Volume II, No. 26, copy in John Carter Brown Library, as having occurred on October 21, 1752. Following this note is his "Character taken from the Boston Evening Post, October 23, 1752."

11. See Appendix X.

12. See Appendix X for a detailed account of Colden's *History of the Five Nations*.

13. The zenith of bibliomania is found in the unfortunate experience of the Johnsonian collector who went mad searching for the folio volume with which, an untrue legend has it, Dr. Johnson beat the impertinent bookseller.

14. Perhaps the most notable of the studies preceding Colden's was

the section on the Tuscaroras in John Lawson's *New Voyage to Carolina*, London, 1709. Lawson died by torture, inflicted by the Indians he had sympathetically described.

15. *History of American Literature*, II, 214.

16. *Colden Papers*, IV, 6.

17. Huske, *Present State of North America*, page 42.

18. *The Yale Review*, July, 1928, pages 749–766.

19. De Puy, *Bibliography of the English Colonial Treaties with the American Indians*, No. 22.

20. *Ibid.*, No. 23.

21. *Ibid.*, No. 19.

22. Compiled by Provost William Smith of the College of Philadelphia. For notes on this book and its reissue with the title *Some Account of the North American Indians*, see Wilberforce Eames in Sabin, Nos. 84671 and 84673. *The Speech of a Creek Indian* was noticed at considerable length, pages 285–293, in the *Monthly Review* for April, 1754. There is reason to believe that Dr. Smith himself wrote this review of his book, for his name is written after it in Griffith's office copy of the *Review*. It is upon this record kept by the editor and publisher that Mr. Benjamin C. Nangle has based his forthcoming book (Clarendon Press) on the contributors to that great periodical.

23. Page 252.

24. Letter of Henry Callister in Lawrence C. Wroth, "A Maryland Merchant and his Friends in 1750," in *Maryland Historical Magazine*, September, 1911, pages 213–240.

25. "Witham Marshe's Journal of the Treaty . . . at Lancaster . . . June, 1744" in *Collections of the Massachusetts Historical Society, for the Year MDCCC*, pages 171–201.

26. *History of the Five Indian Nations*, London, 1747, pages 14–15.

27. Brinton, *Library of Aboriginal American Literature*, No. II (*The Iroquois Book of Rites*), page 117 *et seq.*

28. Work cited in note 19, above, Nos. 44 and 45.

29. Mr. R. W. G. Vail, Librarian of the American Antiquarian Society, has in preparation a definitive bibliography of the Indian Captivities. One finds an extraordinarily rich collection of the Captivities in the Edward E. Ayer Collection of the Newberry Library of Chicago. Its contents are listed in "Publications of the Newberry Library, Number 3," entitled *Narratives of Captivity among the Indians of North America*, Chicago, 1912, a bibliography in which are entered 339

titles. In a supplement to this list issued in 1928, the Newberry Library has added 143 titles.

30. Evans, No. 7160.

31. Evans, No. 8116.

32. Sabin, No. 3868.

33. Weiser's record of the treaty he concluded with the Iroquois on behalf of Virginia is found in *Minutes of the Provincial Council of Pennsylvania*, IV, 660–669.

34. One of the interesting features of the map of 1749 is the tracing of the route of this memorable journey from Philadelphia to Lake Ontario. A long extract from Evans's Journal, all that seems to remain, is found in Thomas Pownall's *Topographical Description*, Appendix Number V, London, 1776, pages 5–6.

35. The full title of Bartram's *Observations* is found in Sabin, No. 3868. Many interesting references to the journey and to the journal, condensed in our text, are found in William Darlington's *Memorials of John Bartram and Humphry Marshall*, Philadelphia, 1849, specifically in the following letters: Bartram to Cadwallader Colden, June 26, 1743, page 328; Bartram to Sir Hans Sloane, September 23, 1743, page 304; Bartram to Peter Collinson, date obliterated, page 169; Peter Collinson to Bartram, undated, page 171; Bartram to Peter Collinson, July 24, 1744, page 172; Bartram to Gronovius, December 6, 1745, page 354. Bartram's *Observations* is entered in the *Gentleman's Magazine* for February, 1751, page 95, among publications of February.

36. Kalm's account of Niagara as found in Bartram's *Observations* was printed in the *Gentleman's Magazine* for January, 1751, pages 15–19. In the February issue following appeared an engraved "View of the Fall of Niagara" intended to illustrate the article. The view traces to the Hennepin prototype through the inset on sheet I of Popple's *Map of the British Empire*, 1733. It resembles very closely the large undated print (copy in John Carter Brown Library), *The Water-fall of Niagara*, "R. Hancock fecit," with legend in English and French.

37. It is this aspect of the Preface that causes one to suppose that Collinson had turned over the Journal to another to edit. But he seems, none the less, to have been concerned in its publication. On January 20, 1751, he wrote to Bartram, "Thy journal is in the press; hope to send it by next ship." (Work cited in note 35, above, page 182.)

38. Kalm, *Travels into North America*, 1770, I, 113–114. This English version was translated and abridged by John Reinhold Forster

from Volumes II–III of the German translation (Göttingen, 3 v., 1754–64) of Kalm's *En Resa til Norra America*, Stockholm, 1753–1761.

39. Thomson's *Enquiry* occupied pages 1–128. Writing to Israel Pemberton on March 19, 1759 (Smyth, *Writings of Benjamin Franklin*, III, 470–472), Franklin said that David Hall would send to him and Mr. Thomson twenty-five copies of "the Enquiries to which Post's first Journal is added, which being more generally interesting occasions the other to go into more hands and be more read." The reviewer of Thomson's *Enquiry* in the *Monthly Review* for June, 1759, in this case Ralph Griffiths, the editor of the *Monthly*, characterized Post's Journal as "a curious, though somewhat tedious account of the success of this honest enthusiast."

40. In Appendix II is quoted more of this letter from Franklin to Israel Pemberton, dated March 19, 1759, referred to in the preceding note, in which occurs the following sentence: "I have just received the copy of Post's second Journal, which will be of good use." The book was published with the title: *Second Journal of Christian Frederick Post, On a Message from the Governor of Pensilvania to the Indians on the Ohio*. London: Printed for J. Wilkie . . . MDCLIX. (Field, *Essay towards an Indian Bibliography*, No. 1233.) It was noticed briefly at the conclusion of the review of Thomson's *Enquiry* in the *Monthly Review* for June, 1759. One supposes Franklin responsible for its publication (just as he was responsible for the first *Journal*) for the reason that the following entry is found in his "Account Book, 1757–1762": "July 12, 1759 . . . also sent to D. Hall 300 of Post's Second Journals. Some of the first were sent him before." (*Pennsylvania Magazine of History and Biography*, LV, No. 2, April, 1931, page 123.) The two "Journals" of Post were reprinted in Proud's *History of Pennsylvania*, 2 v. Philadelphia, 1797–1798, Vol. II. Appendix, Part II, Nos. VIII and IX.

41. The events and negotiations leading up to Post's mission are found in *Pennsylvania Archives*, Volume III, and in the *Minutes of the Provincial Council of Pennsylvania*, Volume VIII.

42. Full title and description in Wilberforce Eames, *The Antigua Press and Benjamin Mecom, 1748–1765*, No. 10, where it is entered in the list of Boston imprints of Mecom. See also Evans, No. 8194, and Wegelin, *Early American Poetry*, No. 269. It was reprinted in an early nineteenth-century edition with the same author's *Conquest of Louisbourg*. See note 44, below.

43. I have not found trace of a published poem by Maylem of this title, but his *Gallic Perfidy*, Boston, 1758, begins, page 7:

> I who of late, in Epic Strains essay'd,
> *And sung the Hero on Acadie's Plains,

and at the foot of the page, the author has placed a footnote with asterisk which reads, "The Conquest of Beau-se-jour, by Colonels Moncton and Winslow, in 1755."

44. The two eighteenth-century and one nineteenth-century editions of *The Conquest of Louisbourg* present bibliographical problems that I am not able to solve now and maybe never, but I have in preparation a separate study of John Maylem and his work, which I hope to complete in the spring of 1934. In that paper I expect to present all that I can find bearing upon the editions of this work. My present knowledge indicates that there was an edition of Boston, 1758; one of Newport, 1775; and an early nineteenth-century reprint in one volume of this poem and the *Gallic Perfidy*.

APPENDIX I

THE ARCHIBALD KENNEDY TRACTS

(The anonymous titles in the ensuing list, enclosed in square brackets, are attributed to Archibald Kennedy on grounds explained in a later section of this Appendix.)

1. Observations on the Importance of the Northern Colonies under Proper Regulations. [*typographical ornament*] New-York: Printed and Sold by James Parker, at the New Printing-Office, in Beaver-Street, 1750.

    8vo. [iv], 1–36. Page [i]: title as above, verso blank; pages [iii–iv]: dedication "To the Right Honourable Henry Pelham, Esq; Chancellor and Under-Treasurer; First Lord Commissioner of the Treasury, and One of His Majesty's Most Honourable Privy-Council.", signed, page [iv]: "Arch. Kennedy."; pages 1–36: "Observations, &c."

2. The Importance of Gaining and Preserving the Friendship of the Indians to the British Interest, considered. [*typographical ornament*] New-York: Printed and Sold by James Parker, at the New Printing-Office, in Beaver-Street, 1751.

    8vo. 1–31. Pages [1–2]: probably leaf containing half-title; page [3]: title as above, verso blank; pages 5–26: "The Importance, &c."; pages 27–31: "The Author of the foregoing Essay, having desired the Printer to communicate the Manuscript to some of the most judicious of his Friends, it produced the following Letter from one of them: The publishing whereof, we think, needs no other Apology, viz. Philadelphia, March 20, 1750, 1. Dear Mr. Parker,"; page 31: "I am, Yours affectionately."

3. The Importance of Gaining and Preserving the Friendship of the Indians to the British Interest considered. [*woodcut ornament*] London: Printed for E. Cave, jun. at St John's Gate. M.DCC.LII.

    8vo. [iv], 1–46. Pages [i–ii]: probably leaf containing half-title; pages [iii–iv]: title as above, verso blank; pages 1–38: "The Importance, &c."; pages 38–46: "The author of the foregoing Essay . . ." [wording as in collation of No. 2, above].

4. [An Essay on the Government of the Colonies. Fitted to the Lati-

tude Forty-one, but may, without sensible Error, serve all the Northern Colonies. Poor Richard's Title-Page. [*typographical ornament*] New-York: Printed and Sold by J. Parker, at the New Printing-Office in Beaver-Street, 1752.]

Sm. 8vo. 1–42. Page 1: title as above, verso blank; pages 3–42: "An Essay, &c."

5. Serious Considerations on the Present State of the Affairs of the Northern Colonies. [*ornament*] New-York: Printed for the Author. 1754.

8vo. 1–24. Page 1: title as above, verso blank; pages 3–24: "Serious Considerations, &c."

6. Serious Considerations on the Present State of the Affairs of the Northern Colonies. By Archibald Kennedy, Esq; Author of the Importance of Gaining and Preserving the Friendship of the Indians of the Six Nations, to the British Interest, considered. [*ornament*] New-York, Printed: London, Reprinted for R. Griffiths, at the Dunciad, in Pater-noster Row. [1754.]

8vo. 1–24. Page 1: title as above; page 2: advertisement by R. Griffiths, 1754, of *Some Account of the North-America* [*sic*] *Indians* (see our text note 22, Chapter III); pages 3–24: "Serious Considerations, &c."

7. [Serious Advice to the Inhabitants of the Northern-Colonies, on the Present Situation of Affairs. [*ornament, same as in No. 5, above*] New-York: Printed for the Author, 1755.]

8vo. 1–20. Page 1: title as above, verso blank; pages 3–20: "Serious Advice, &c."

8. [A Speech Said to have been Delivered Some Time Before the Close of the Last Sessions, By a Member Dissenting from The Church. [*typographical ornament*] Printed in the Year 1755.]

Sm. 8vo. 1–52. Page 1: title as above, verso blank; pages 3–38: "A Speech, &c."; pages 39–52: "To the Albany Members. From their Constituents."

THE TRACTS

1. In the *New York Post-Boy* for March 21, 1765, John Holt, Parker's partner then in charge of the New York establishment, inserted the following notice:

"In the Year 1750, a Pamphlet was wrote and printed in this City, entitled, *Observations on the Importance of the Northern Colonies under proper Regulations*; dedicated and designed to be presented to the Right Honourable Henry Pelham, Esq; but that

Gentleman dying soon after it was printed, the Pamphlet never was published, and but a very few of the worthy Author's Friends ever saw it; now as the Purport Matter of the Pamphlet has been thought to be of Importance, and has some Relation to a Scheme said to be on Foot in Britain, for using of American Timber in the Royal Navy; the Printer thereof having never been paid for printing it, has taken this Method to offer it yet for Sale to the Curious; and is to be sold at the Printing Office near the Exchange in New-York, Price 1 s."

I have not been able to determine the real reason for the failure of this tract to attain publication at the time it was printed. The statement of circumstances made by Holt in the notice just quoted is certainly incorrect in giving Pelham's death as the reason the tract was not published in 1750, for that statesman did not die until March, 1754. The printer's failure to receive payment for this tract does not seem to constitute a reflection upon Mr. Kennedy, who is referred to in the advertisement quoted above as "the worthy Author." Furthermore in the next five years Parker printed for him certainly No. 2 of the tracts listed above, and probably Nos. 4, 5, and 7 as well.

2. Advertised as "just published" in *The New York Gazette revived in the Weekly Post-Boy* for May 6, 1751, and repeated in the issue of May 13th. In the following extract from a letter to Cadwallader Colden (*Colden Papers*, IV, 264), Kennedy explains the purpose of the book and makes clear Benjamin Franklin's authorship of the letter to the printer occupying pages 27–31 of the tract:

Dear Sir   15th Ap. 1751

I once told you I had got some confused ideas of Indian affairs in my head, they are now before you, and submitted to your better Judgement and correction, my friends have advised the publishing of them with Mr. Franklands remarks, to which he has agreed absque nomine This however, will depend in a great measure upon what you will please to advise. If you approve I hope I shall have your observations, and the sooner the better that they appear (if they appear at all) in a proper shape at the Grand Congress at Albany in June next. . . .

Dear Sir
Most humbly yours
Arch^d Kennedy

This piece was first recognized as Franklin's by Professor Edward

Eggleston who called it to the attention of John Bigelow when he was editing *The Complete Works of Benjamin Franklin*, where this interesting fact is recorded, III, 217n. Mr. Bigelow accepted Professor Eggleston's attribution because the piece bore "so many distinct traces of Franklin's authorship." He reprinted it, therefore, from the tract. Ford, *Franklin Bibliography*, Nos. 85 and 86, accepted it as Franklin's on the basis of its inclusion by Bigelow. The letter quoted above is the only contemporary reference I have found that makes certain the correctness of Professor Eggleston's attribution.

Contemporary printed evidence of Kennedy's authorship of the tract is found on the title-page of No. 6.

3. The collation given by Ford, *Franklin Bibliography*, No. 86, repeats that of his No. 85 and is incorrect for this edition. This English edition of the book was noticed briefly in the *Monthly Review* for February, 1752, page 150.

4. See in the next section below, reasons for attributing this tract to Kennedy. The copy in the John Carter Brown Library, bought from Henry Stevens, Son & Stiles in 1914, is the only one I have been able so far to locate. I have not been able to find a notice of its publication in any New York newspaper, but a nearly contemporary reference to it is cited in text note No. 77.

5. Advertised as "just published" in *The New York Gazette: or, the Weekly Post-Boy* for August 12, 1754. See title No. 6 for contemporary revelation of authorship. It was probably printed by James Parker. It resembles Parker's work and it was advertised in his newspaper as noted above, and as long afterwards as March 22, 1756, it was offered in his newspaper in a group of three publications of which one certainly was from his press.

6. Noticed in *Monthly Review* for October, 1754, page 316.

7. It is under the title *Advice to the Inhabitants of the Northern Colonies* that this book seems to be entered, anonymously, in Evans, No. 7347, without location of a copy or indication of the source from which the title was obtained. I have not found an advertisement of it in a New York newspaper. In addition to a copy of the *Serious Advice, etc.* belonging to Mr. Lathrop C. Harper, inscribed on title-page "Chad (?) Hamersley New York," copies are to be found in the New York Historical Society and the Library Company of Philadelphia, but not elsewhere, as so far discovered. Mr. Harper first suggested to me Kennedy's authorship of this anonymous tract, and I have given in the section below reasons for accepting his attribution as highly probable.

8. Advertised as "just published" in the *New York Mercury* for February 17, 1755. On the last page is a design made up of printers' ornaments of which some—the rose, the thistle, and the crown—and probably all, are identical with those normally used by Hugh Gaine. On the title-page is a typographical flower used elsewhere by Gaine and in the same arrangement as here employed. The appearance of the advertisement in the *Mercury*, and these specific and general typographical resemblances to other works by Gaine, make it seem reasonable to attribute the book to his press. The only copy of this book I have seen bears on its title-page a contemporary attribution of its authorship to Archibald Kennedy. In the section below this inscription is quoted and reasons are given for believing its attribution of authorship to be correct.

THE AUTHORSHIP OF THE ANONYMOUS TRACTS

Of these six tracts, three, *i.e.*, Nos. 4, 7, and 8, have not been attributed hitherto to Archibald Kennedy. The reasons for the attribution of the three anonymous pamphlets to this intelligent New York conservative rest upon a study of the contents of all six tracts in conjunction with one another. In the course of this examination the purpose was to trace through all the tracts similarity in political sentiments, the repetition of general and specific ideas, and method of exposition rather than identities in language. Before presenting the table in which the result of the examination is displayed, certain general statements may be made. All the tracts, for example, display conservatism in contrast to the anti-governmental sentiments of the popular, or Assembly, party then active in most of the Middle Colonies. The Indian question has prominent place in all, and the point of view expressed toward it is invariably that of conciliation of the tribes by greater consideration of their needs in peace and war. Characteristic features in method of exposition in all are the use of anecdote, fable, and allegory, and a notable employment of illustration by long passages quoted from ancient and modern authors. A legitimate objection to conclusions based upon a similarity in ideas throughout a series of pamphlets is that ideas soon become common property and are normally found repeated in the writings of contemporaries, sometimes borrowed one from another, sometimes the expression and reiteration of prevailing notions. In the present case, however, so many of the ideas are specific and so many are known to have been first given public emphasis by Kennedy, and they are presented so often in a style distinctly his that this objection is to some extent weakened.

Ideas & Projects	Observations on the Northern Colonies 1750	Importance of Friendship of Indians 1751	Serious Considerations on Northern Colonies 1754	Essay on Government of Colonies 1752	Serious Advice to Northern Colonies 1755	A Speech said to have been delivered 1755
	Page	Page	Page	Page	Page	Page
Establishment of a system of alarms and signals for Hudson Valley and Long Island		10, 25				51
Strategic importance of New York City, Albany, & Hudson Valley	6	7, 17	6		12, 16	29, 35, 41+
Plan of fortification of New York City		23				41
Emphasis on Indians as balance of Power and on establishing proper relations	6	Through-out	8+	37, 39	16	46
Demolition of certain fortifications now existing in Indian country as a measure of gaining confidence of natives			20			48
Discussion of trade between Albany and Canada		Through-out	18–19	39		49
Application of a law of Charles II concerning nationality of traders			20	40		
Importance of regaining friendship of Cachnawaga tribe, and explanation that Iroquois would not fight against these relatives of the Mohawks		11	19			49
Proposal of tax or quit rent			17	35, 37–38		
Suggestion of barrier colonies		8–9			15	

Ideas & Projects	Observations on the Northern Colonies 1750	Importance of Friendship of Indians 1751	Serious Considerations on Northern Colonies 1754	Essay on Government of Colonies 1752	Serious Advice to Northern Colonies 1755	A Speech said to have been delivered 1755
	Page	Page	Page	Page	Page	Page
Proposal to garrison and colonize Scotch Highlanders, a race with affinities to the Indians		8	12		15	
Uselessness of regular troops and regular military methods in forest warfare			6		5–6, 14	
Need of a union of the colonies		8, 18+	6		6–7	33
Defense of Governors against Assemblies				41		9
Criticism and exhortation of Assemblies	7	21–22, 26	14, 17	Through-out	15	31, 36, 38+
Conviction that victory of France meant slavery of British			3, 8		3, 9, 13, 20	33, 34
Danger in British, in spite of numerical preponderance, trying to fight the French by separate colonies, but ease of victory if united, and if Indians were properly managed		6			3–5	33–34
Crown not to be put to expense of defending colonies, but fund to be raised by a pro-rata assessment of the several colonies		7			6–7	32+
Fables or old stories employed by way of illustration			14, 17, 24		7–8	24, 26, 29–31
Si quid novisti rectius, candidus imperti	12					52

The foregoing analysis of the ideas and projects in the six tracts may be summarized as follows:

In the *Essay on the Government of the Colonies*, the work of one who is obviously a strong government man, are found five instances in which are mentioned, or discussed at length, ideas that appear in one or more of the tracts published under Kennedy's name. Two of these, the proposal to apply a law of Charles II forbidding aliens to engage in British trade, and the proposal of a land tax or quit rent to defray the costs of defense are specific in character. The remaining ideas common to this tract and others are more general in character. They were not peculiar to Kennedy, but nevertheless they are emphasized in all his acknowledged writings. A sixth idea in the *Essay*, the defense of the governor against the assembly, appears also in *A Speech, etc.*, the only one of the anonymous tracts (see below) for which there seems to exist a contemporary attribution to Kennedy.

In the *Serious Advice to the Inhabitants of the Northern Colonies*, written by one distrustful of the Assemblies, are found at least eleven cases of ideas and projects appearing in Kennedy's acknowledged tracts. One of these is specific, and, so far as I have observed, peculiar to Kennedy; that is, the proposal to create a barrier colony of Scotch Highlanders, alleging their affinity to the Indians in manners and way of living. These tracts were written, it may be observed, before Walter Scott had romanticized the Highlander. Kennedy himself was of a noble Highland family and presumably knew what he was talking about. The similarity in title between this and Kennedy's *Serious Considerations on the Affairs of the Northern Colonies* of the preceding year may also be taken into account.

In *A Speech said to have been Delivered, etc.*, a tract in which again appears an anti-Assembly bias, are found fourteen cases in which are expressed ideas of one or more of the acknowledged Kennedy tracts. Of these, five are specific in character; namely, the establishment of a system of alarms, a plan for the fortification of New York City, the demolition of certain fortified places in the Indian country, a statement of the necessity of regaining the friendship of the Cachnawaga Indians, and the repetition of an uncommon Latin phrase to illustrate a similar idea. The only known copy of this tract, now belonging to Mr. Lathrop C. Harper of New York, bears in a contemporary hand, in the place usually occupied by the author's name, "by Archibald Kennedy, Esqʳ", and at the foot of the page an inscription of two lines or more, barbarously ploughed by a binder, of which may be read only the words "Mr Kennedy shewed this in Mss. to James Alexa . . ." Under date of July 19, 1933, Mr. Alexander J. Wall, Librarian of the New York Historical Society, wrote me as follows concerning this title-page inscription, submitted to him in a photostat copy of the page: "I should say without hesitation that the writing on the title-page . . . is that of James Alexander. We have many boxes of his manuscripts here." There could hardly be better contemporary evidence for the attribution of the pamphlet to Archibald Kennedy than the assertion of his long-time associate, James Alexander, who at the time of publication of the *Speech, etc.*, was a member of the Council of the Province of New York.

It would be too much to claim that the attribution of these three tracts to Archibald Kennedy had been established beyond doubt by the foregoing analysis of their contents, but no other aspirant for the honor of having written them has been suggested and the examination here described has shown that they express Kennedy's government-servant point of view, his general and specific ideas, and his method of exposition. I may add that in making this examination I found nothing in the anonymous tracts in the least contrary to Kennedy's sentiments and beliefs so far as these are known to me.

APPENDIX II

[CHARLES THOMSON], ENQUIRY
INTO THE ALIENATION OF
THE INDIANS

---

1. An Enquiry into the Causes of the Alienation of the Delaware and Shawanese Indians from the British Interest, And into Measures taken for recovering their Friendship . . . Written in Pensylvania. London: Printed for J. Wilkie, at the Bible, in St. Paul's Church-yard. MDCCLIX.

    8vo. 1–184. Page [1]: title, verso blank; pages 3–6: "The Intro-duction."; pages 7–128: "An Enquiry, &c."; pages 129–184: "Appendix.", comprising (pages 130–171) "The Journal of Christian Frederick Post . . ."; (pages 172–182) "Extract of a Letter from Philadelphia, dated Dec. 10, 1758"; (pages 183–184) "Extract of a Letter from one of the Friendly Association in Philadelphia, dated December 11, 1758." "A Map of the Province of Pensylvania. intended chiefly to Illustrate . . . the Indian Purchases . . . T. Jefferys sculp."

AUTHORSHIP OF THE "ENQUIRY" AND ITS
SEVERAL PARTS

    The attribution of this book to Charles Thomson seems to have been by common consent derived from knowledge of the part taken by Thomson in the events which produced it. There exist, however, in certain unpublished Franklin letters two contemporary references to the book which put the question of its authorship beyond doubt. These are quoted here through the courtesy of their respective owners.

    Writing to Joseph Galloway from London on February 17, 1758, Franklin said:

    "The Indian Treaty under the Great Seal, Mr. Hunt thinks is also in his chest; it is not, however, yet come to hand. But Mr. Thomson's piece on the Causes of the Indians' Uneasiness he has just received, and I am to have a sight of it." (From an unpublished letter in the posses-

sion of Mr. William Smith Mason of Evanston, Illinois. Extract communicated to me by Mr. George Simpson Eddy of New York.)

More than a year later, on April 12, 1759, Franklin wrote from
London to Mrs. Franklin as follows:

"Tell Mr. Thomson that I have just heard the Proprietor is writing
an Answer to his Book, and will pay off him and the Quakers." (From
an unpublished letter in the American Philosophical Society collection
of Franklin Papers, *Calendar*, III, 448, document XLVI, ii, 14.)

From another letter, Franklin to Israel Pemberton, a founder of the
Friendly Association, dated March 19, 1759 (Smyth, *Writings of Ben-
jamin Franklin*, III, 470–472), we learn the authorship of the two
supplementary communications, which, with Post's *Journal*, make up the
Enquiry. From comparison of dates it appears that the long letter of
December 10, 1758, was written by Thomson, and the shorter one of
December 11 by Pemberton himself. Franklin wrote to Pemberton as
follows: "I received your favour of Dec. 11 and Jan^{ry} 19. by those
Ships you will receive some of the printed Enquiries to which Post's
first Journal is added, which being more generally interesting occasions
the other to go into more Hands and be more read. Extracts of your and
Mr Thomson's Letters are also added to make the Thing more com-
pleat. M[r.] Hall has orders to deliver twenty five to you and M^r
Thomson; and I hope you will promote the Sale of the rest, that the
Charges of Printing etc. may be lessen'd."

THE COMPOSITION OF THE BOOK

The book had its origin in the activities of a body of Pennsylvania
Quakers known as "The Friendly Association for Regaining and Preserving Peace with the Indians by Pacific Measures." This organization,
of which Charles Thomson was a member, began an investigation into
the Indian affairs of the Province as early as 1756. Its address, *To
William Denny, Esquire, Lieutenant Governor of Pennsylvania*, dated
at the end, "Philadelphia, the 14th of the Seventh Month, 1757,"
gives a history of the movement that has particular bearing upon Thomson's *Enquiry*. (This address, printed at Philadelphia probably in
August or September, 1757, see letter of Conrad Weiser of October 27,
1757, *Pennsylvania Archives*, III, 313–314, is very rare in its contemporary printed form. Its two leaves in folio contain the address as found
in the *Minutes of the Provincial Council of Pennsylvania*, VII, 638–646,
where it is dated the "13th 7 mo" instead of the 14th. On pages 637,
647–648 of the work just cited are found also documents relating to

the address in which the Governor virtually forbids its publication as tending to inflame the minds of the Indians, then gathering for the Treaty at Easton, and in which the Friendly Association agrees to postpone publication for "a few Days." It seems likely that it was not published, indeed, until after the conclusion of that Treaty on August 7th, for it was only a few weeks before October 27th that a copy of the printed address came into the hands of Conrad Weiser, who would most certainly have seen it if it had been published during the Treaty.) The address asserted that following the attacks of the Indians upon the borders of the Province in the winter of 1755–1756, the public had waited in vain for the Government to make enquiry into the "Causes which induc'd our antient steady Friends to become our Enemies," but that instead of this course being pursued, "Great Military Preparations were . . . made and Forts erected in many Parts of the Frontiers . . ."; that even after the Governor had gained the confidence of Teedyuscung at the Easton Treaty of 1756, and had learned from him that the Indians felt themselves badly used in the matter of certain land purchases, nothing had been done in the way of searching the provincial records in order to bring out the actual facts of the land transactions of the past. In view of these circumstances, the Friendly Association had regarded themselves, as they said, "under the strongest Obligations, to make all the Enquiry in our Power, into the true State of the Indian Claims," and this they had done or were then doing "tho' the Secretary refus'd to permit us to proceed therein, by inspecting the Records in his Office. . . ."

At the Treaty at Easton in 1757, despite the Governor's opposition to the appointment of a clerk or secretary for Teedyuscung, the Delaware chieftain, such appointment was made in the person of Charles Thomson. On August 4, 1757 (*Pennsylvania Archives*, III, 256), Thomson wrote to Governor Denny in terms that indicate he was already engaged in a thorough study of the Indian affairs of the Province. (See also *Minutes of the Provincial Council*, VII, 724.) Thomson's minutes of the Easton conference, differing in some essentials from the official record of the proceedings, were ordered by the Assembly to be sent to England to the colonial agents of whom Franklin was the chief (*V & P of the Pennsylvania Assembly*, Miller edition, IV, 749, September 29, 1757), together with documents supporting the Indian claim, Teedyuscung having asked that the whole matter be referred to the King for arbitration. In a letter earlier cited, Franklin under date of February 17, 1758, wrote to Joseph Galloway: "Their [*i.e.*, the

Indians'] complaints are now in the hands of the Ministry, but when they will have leisure to consider them, God only knows. For tho' securing the affections of the Indians, by doing them justice, be a matter of great consequence, they have other affairs at present on their hands that seem to them of more immediate importance."

THE PUBLICATION OF THE "ENQUIRY"

It was in the letter just quoted from that Franklin told Galloway he was to be allowed a sight of "Mr. Thomson's piece on the Causes of the Indians' Uneasiness." This is the first we learn of Thomson having put into book form the results of his enquiry, or rather of the enquiry undertaken by him on behalf of the Friendly Association. It is evident that the sight Franklin had of the manuscript gave him a good deal of satisfaction. He recognized its value as an agency in arraying public and official opinion against the Penns, his chief reason for being in England at that time, and he seems then or soon afterwards to have undertaken its editing and publication. This becomes apparent in the words quoted above from his letter to Israel Pemberton of March 19, 1759, and from this passage in a letter to David Hall, his partner in the Philadelphia printing house, dated April 8, 1759, found in Smyth, *Writings of Benjamin Franklin*, III, 478: "Billy has sent you in the 2 Vessels which lately sai'd for Philad^a 300 of the Enquirys 50 of which are to be deliver'd to the Assembly, 25 to Isr^l Pemberton & Charles Thomson, and the remaining 225 to be dispos'd of in Pensylvania and the neighbouring Governments." (A copy of the book in the John Carter Brown Library bears the following inscription on its title-page: "Samuel Gould's Book Bought at David Halls the 29th Day of the 6 mo called June 1759.") Finally on April 7, 1759, Franklin wrote Galloway (unpublished letter belonging to Mr. William Smith Mason, but see his article "The Franklin-Galloway Correspondence" in the *Proceedings of the American Antiquarian Society*, October, 1924, page 252):

"The Enquiry into the Causes of the Alienation of the Shawanese and Delaware Indians has been some time published, and is more read than I expected. It will, I think have a good effect."

There is every reason to believe from the evidence adduced that Franklin on behalf of the Province had assumed financial responsibility for the publication, but I have not been able to find record of a payment to a printer for the book itself in the *Account Book of Benjamin Franklin, 1757–1762*, published by George Simpson Eddy in the *Pennsylvania Magazine of History and Biography*, LV, No. 2, April, 1931.

But in that record, under date of May 11, 1759, I find the following pertinent entry: "Paid Jefferies, engraver, for Indian map £ 4 – 19 s – o d." This must be the "Map of the Province of Pensylvania intended chiefly to Illustrate the Indian Purchases. T. Jefferys sculp." which forms an important feature of Thomson's *Enquiry*.

Though the book was not reviewed in the *Monthly Review* until June, 1759, it is clear from the date of Franklin's letter to Israel Pemberton, quoted above, that it was published, or certainly in print, before March 19th of that year.

THE VALUE OF THE "ENQUIRY"

Though a strongly partisan statement in which humanitarianism and political expediency were curiously mingled, the book, as shown in the foregoing text, was an effective contemporary influence, and is today an important document for the historian who would understand the period. It is worth while correcting the statement concerning it made by Justin Winsor, *Narrative and Critical History*, V, 575, in which, referring to Winthrop Sargent's *History of Braddock's Expedition*, page 55, the historian wrote of the *Enquiry* as "a volume of greater rarity than of value, in Sargent's opinion." Following out the reference, one finds that Sargent's opinion was actually very different from Winsor's understanding of it. He frequently cites the *Enquiry* as authority, and in a note on the page designated by Winsor wrote: "This volume, whose rarity is greater than even its value and importance, was the work of Charles Thomson. . . ." The contemporary effectiveness of the book was immediately recognized, judging from Franklin's report to Galloway, quoted above, from the irritation it caused Thomas Penn, and, as commented upon in the text, from the review of it which Ralph Griffiths, the editor and publisher of the *Monthly Review*, wrote in his issue of June, 1759, pages 545–548.

APPENDIX III

JOHN HUSKE, THE PRESENT STATE OF NORTH AMERICA, PART I

1. The present State of North America, &c. Part I. [*publisher's mono-gram*] London: Printed for, and Sold by R. and J. Dodsley in Pall-mall. MDCCLV.

    4to. [i–iv], 1–88. Page [i]: title, verso blank; pages [iii–iv]: "The Contents.", comprising the heads of Chapters I–VIII; pages 1–88: text, comprising Chapters I–III, only; page 88: twelve lines of text, "The End of the Third Chapter.", three lines headed "Errata.", and "N.B. The rest of this Work will be published with all possible Dispatch."

2. The present State of North America. Lately presented to the Lords of the Regency of Great-Britain. Part. I. [*printer's monogram*] Dublin: Printed by George Faulkner, in Essex-street. MDCCLV.

    8vo. [i–viii], 1–72. Page [i]: probably half-title, verso blank; page [iii]: title, verso blank; pages [v–vii]: "The Contents.", comprising the heads of Chapters I–VIII; page [viii]: blank; pages 1–72: text, comprising Chapters I–III, only; page 72: "The End of the Third Chapter.", followed by "N.B. The Rest of the Work will be published with all possible Dispatch."

3. The Present State of North-America. [*nine lines containing the heads of Chapters I, II, and III*] [*type ornament*] London, Printed 1755. Boston, New England, Re-printed and Sold by D. Fowle in Ann Street, and by Z. Fowle in Middle-street. 1755.

    8vo. [i–ii], 1–64, [65–66]. Page [i]: title, verso blank; pages 1–64: text, comprising Chapters I–III, only; page 64: "The End of the Third Chapter.", followed by "The Author of the fore-going gives Notice, that the rest of this Work will be published with all possible Dispatch in London; and as we may expect the other Copy by the first Vessel from thence, it will be published here for the great Benefit to the Plantations in general."; page

[65]: advertisement of D. Fowle of William Douglass's *Summary of the British Settlements in North-America*; page [66]: blank.

4. The present State of North America, &c. Part I. The Second Edition, with Emendations. [*publisher's monogram.*] London: Printed for, and Sold by R. and J. Dodsley in Pall-mall. MDCCLV.

> 4to. Collation as in first edition except page 88, which is as follows: ten lines of text; "The End of the Third Chapter."; "N.B. The rest of this Work will be published with all possible Dispatch, with an accurate Map of the Country, shewing the Rights of Great-Britain, France, and Spain."

5. The Present State of North-America. [*nine lines as in first Boston edition*] N.B. This Book has been in such great Demand, that it has had two Editions already this Year in England, and this is the second Edition in Boston. And by the best Judges of the Affairs of this Country, it is thought to be peculiarly seasonable at this time, and is worthy the Perusal of every true Englishman. London, Printed 1755. Boston, New-England, Re-printed and Sold by D. Fowle in Ann-Street, and by Z. Fowle in Middle-street. 1755.

> 8vo. [i–ii], 1–64, [65–66]. Collation by pages as in first Boston edition.

6. Allgemeine Amerikanische Kriegsgeschichte, an den Flüssen Ohio, St. Laurenz, St. Johann, &c. Oder: Gründliche Nachricht von den Angelegenheiten der Grosbrittanischen und Französischen Kronen, in Ansehung des gegenwärtigen Krieges in Nordamerika. Aus dem Englischen übersetzt, mit einer dazu gehörigen Landkarte und Kupferstich begleitet, und heraus gegeben von H.V.W. Frankfurt und Leipzig, 1755.

> Sm. 8vo. I–XVIII, 1–121, [122–124]; 2 plates, map.

7. Title and collation as above in No. 6, but with date "1756."

8. Geographische und historisch-politische Nachrichten von demjenigen Theil des Nördlichen Amerika, um dessen Gränzen, zwischen den Franzosen und Engländern, gegenwärtig Krieg geführet wird. Nebst einer Beschreibung der dasigen vortheilhaften Handlung und Beschaffenheit des Landes, besonders was Neuland oder Terreneuve, Akadien oder Neuschottland, Neuengland, Pensilvanien, Philadelfia, Carolina, Georgien, U.S.W. betrift. Aus dem Französischen übersetzt, und mit der Nordamerikanischen Kriegs-Geschichte, von englischer Seite herausgegeben, begleitet. Mit Kupfern und einer Landcharte versehen. Frankfurt und Leipzig, 1756.

Sm. 8vo. Folding title-page, [i–xx], 1–238; I–XVIII, 1–121, [122–124]; 2 plates, map. See *Catalogue of the De Renne Georgia Library*, I, 136–137.

9. [in a cartouche]: A New and Accurate Map of North America, (wherein the Errors of all preceeding British, French and Dutch Maps, respecting the rights of Great Britain, France & Spain, & the Limits of each of His Majesty's Provinces, are Corrected) Humbly Inscribed to the Honorable Charles Townshend one of the Right Honorable Lords Commissioners for Executing the Office of Lord High Admiral of Great Britain &c. By his Most Obliged, most Obedient and Very Humble Servant Huske. [*at bottom*]: Published for the Present State of North America &c And sold by R. & I. Dodsley in Pall-mall 1755. Tho: Kitchin Sculp^t.
15¾ × 19½ inches.

TIME OF COMPOSITION AND PUBLICATION OF THE
FIRST EDITION

1. The author of the *Present State* refers in the text of its first edition to three publications and a political event which make it possible to fix the period in which the book was being written, namely:

(a) Mitchell's *Map of the British Colonies*
Published February 13, 1755. See discussion of this title in the foregoing text.

(b) William Smith, *A Brief State of Pennsylvania*
Published in February, 1755. See this title in Appendix IV.

(c) *State of the British and French Colonies*
Published in April or May, 1755. See Chapter I, note 54. On page 41 of the *Present State*, its author writes ". . . this very Week a Pamphlet has been published, called the *State of the British and French Colonies, etc.*"

(d) On page 74 of the *Present State*, the author quotes from his Majesty's "late Speech to Parliament." The quotation contains certain sentences found in the *Gentleman's Magazine* for April, 1755, page 184, as part of a speech delivered from the throne on Friday, April 25, 1755.

It is clear from the sense of section (d) above that the *Present State* was being written, or added to in press, later than April 25, 1755.

The book is entered in the *Gentleman's Magazine* for May, 1755, page 238, among books published in May. It was reviewed, probably by Sir Tanfield Leman (information from Benjamin C. Nangle, Yale University) in the *Monthly Review* for June, 1755.

We shall return to the dates thus established, especially to the period of the book's composition, in the section below on the authorship of the *Present State*.

AUTHORSHIP

The *Present State* must have been originally attributed to one of the Huske family for the reason that the map, intended to be issued with Part II (see above, title No. 4), bears the legend "Published for the Present State of North America &c.", and a dedication to Charles Townshend, one of the Lords of the Admiralty, signed simply "Huske." The copy of the second edition in the John Carter Brown Library is in a contemporary calf binding with original end papers and an original label on the back which reads: Huske / North / America. One judges from this fact that the attribution of authorship to an individual named Huske is virtually as old as the book itself. On the fly-leaf of this same copy is a notation in an early, but not necessarily a contemporaneous, hand to the effect that the book had been written by John Hushe, not "Huske." On the authority of this notation the book was catalogued in the old John Carter Brown Catalogue as by "John Hushe," but Sabin, No. 34027, and others following, have corrected the spelling to Huske. The matter of authorship is complicated further by the fact that the new edition of the *British Museum Catalogue* under heading "America, North"; the *Dictionary of National Biography*, article "Huske, Ellis" (1700–1755); and Evans's *American Bibliography*, No. 7434, attribute the book to Ellis Huske, New Hampshire judge, postmaster of Boston, and father of John Huske. In the preceding section, however, it has been shown that the book was written as well as published in England, and that it was still in process of composition after April 25, 1755. It is known, however (see Albert Matthews in *Publications of the Colonial Society of Massachusetts*, IX, 468, quoting the *London Magazine*, June, 1755, page 301), that Ellis Huske died in Boston on April 24, 1755. These circumstances eliminate Ellis Huske from consideration as the possible author of the book. His younger son, Ellis Huske, Jr., seems to have no history and has never been spoken of in connection with the book. We seem compelled, therefore, to fall back upon his elder son, John Huske, as its probable author.

John Huske, son of Ellis, was of American birth. His father was married in 1720 (*Publications of the Colonial Society of Massachusetts*, IX, 467) and it is supposed that John was born in 1721. We learn from his own statement (*Providence Gazette*, November 3, 1764) that he had lived in America for twenty-four years. If the year of his birth is correctly given, this would fix the year 1745 as the time of his removal to England, where, as the nephew of Lieutenant General John Huske, he was probably not without friends. There he remained, engaged in political affairs, until his death in 1773. He was a member of Parliament, representing Malden, Essex, for several years after 1764. An unfriendly contemporary witness, Joseph Reed, wrote in 1764 that Charles Townshend had been his patron. (William B. Reed, *Life and Correspondence of Joseph Reed*, I, 32–33.)

I am indebted for the following facts and argument to the generosity of Professor Verner W. Crane, of the University of Michigan, who is tracing the activities of Huske in connection with a larger study:

In the *Providence Gazette*, November 3, 1764, and the *Boston Gazette* of the next day appeared a letter, dated August 14, 1764, from John Huske, in England, defending himself against the accusation (printed in the *Newport Mercury*, April 9, 1764, and the *Providence Gazette*, April 14, 1764) of having been the person who suggested to the Ministry the imposition of the Stamp Duties upon the colonies. Certain ideas of colonial economic policy enunciated in the letter here referred to provide a parallel to ideas upon that subject found in the *Present State*. On pages 82–83 of the book, for example, are given the heads of a fiscal scheme for the improvement of relations between Great Britain and the colonies which the writer promised to develop in the proposed, but never published, Part II of his work. In his letter of defense printed in the American newspapers of November, 1764, Huske wrote of "a plan I had drawn up several years ago, and is now intended to be printed with observations on the late act," and proceeds to give in very brief and general form an outline of a system of trade regulation that would benefit both Great Britain and the colonies financially, stamp out illicit trade, and alter the burdensome features of the navigation acts. In both the book and the letter appear in one case a striking identity of language in the words "injudicious and destructive imposts and restrictions," but in general the resemblance is one of fundamental ideas rather than of phraseology. This "plan . . . now intended to be printed" seems never to have appeared, or certainly not yet to have been identified. On November 1, 1765, however, John Huske drew up a report, still in manuscript, Public Record Office, Chatham Papers, Bundle 97, also C.O. 5:66, p. 127; and Newcastle Papers, 33030, f. 318, entitled "Observations on the Trade of Great Britain to her Colonies, and their Trade to Foreign Plantations." It is possible that this is the "plan" promised by Huske in his letter printed in November, 1764, but like Part II of the *Present State*, it is not known to have been published.

SUMMARY OF THE CASE FOR JOHN HUSKE

The case for John Huske's authorship of the *Present State* may thus be summarized:

The name "Huske" at the conclusion of the dedication of the map seems to provide a good basis for the assumption that someone of that name was the author of the book with which the map is associated.

The name "Huske" on the contemporary binder's label on the John Carter Brown copy of the second edition of the book is evidence of the early acceptance of its authorship by someone of that name.

The possibilities seem limited to Ellis and John Huske, but the date of the book's completion in London (after April 25, 1755) precludes the idea of its having been written by Ellis, who died in Boston on April 24, 1755.

The map signed "Huske" is dedicated to Charles Townshend, *said by Joseph Reed, writing in 1764, to have been at an earlier time John Huske's patron.*

John Huske was active at this time in English politics and was in the way of writing such a book. Professor Crane points out that according to a letter of John Huske's of November, 1764, it was "several years" before that date that he had drawn up a "plan" for a colonial fiscal policy, and in his brief description of that plan in the letter are strong resemblances to certain proposals on pages 82–83 of the *Present State*, and, in one instance, an absolute identity of language.

The evidence produced is not conclusive, but assuming, as may fairly be done under the circumstances, someone named Huske as the author of the *Present State*, all additional facts brought out point to that individual as being John Huske, merchant, politician, expert in American affairs, and supporter of Franklin in his examination on the Stamp Act before the House of Commons in February, 1766.

THE LATER EDITIONS

2. The text of the Dublin edition follows the first London edition, so that its publication probably occurred before that of the second London edition. The Dublin edition is of particular interest because it alone suggests that the *Present State* had possessed in its inception and purpose an official association. Its title-page carries the statement:

"Lately presented to the Lords of the Regency of Great Britain." A notice in the *Gentleman's Magazine* for April, 1755, page 185, informs us that during the King's absence abroad, "The following persons are appointed lords justices. . . ." Among the Privy Council Papers for March 25, 1752 (Information in letter dated May 29, 1933, from Miss Alice J. Mayes, searcher in the Public Record Office), is a list of Lords of the Regency appointed from the Lords Justices for the period of the King's absence in Hanover. Doubtless the procedure of March, 1752, was followed when the King again went abroad in April, 1755. Unfortunately the Lords of the Regency, having no permanent constitutional standing, did not preserve its papers in any official series. The following series in the Public Record Office have been searched fruitlessly in the hope of turning up a document resembling the *Present State* or a reference to its receipt: Privy Council Papers, 1754–1755; State Papers Domestic, 1752–1755; Colonial Office Papers; Chatham Papers; and several likely sets of Historical Manuscript Commission Reports. There seems nothing to do but accept the statement of the Dublin title-page without learning under what circumstances and in what form the document was presented to the Lords of the Regency.

(3) (5) In the Preface to William Clarke's *Observations on the Conduct of the French* (advertised as "just published" in the *Boston Weekly News-Letter*, August 21, 1755), the author wrote: "the first Part of a Treatise upon the present state of North-America, lately published in London . . . did not come into my Hands, till the greatest Part of this was printed off." Although Clarke's text was written mainly in the closing months of 1754, internal evidence indicates that his dedication to Shirley and the Preface here referred to were written as late as July, 1755. This fact suggests that it was sometime in the summer of 1755 that the first London edition of the *Present State* reached the Boston booksellers. It was not until September 8, 1755, that the first Boston edition of the book was advertised as "just published" in the *Boston Evening Post*. I have found no reference to the second Boston edition in newspaper advertisements, but in the light of the note on its title-page it may be taken for granted that it followed closely upon the first. It seems, indeed, that the type of the first had not been fully distributed before the printing of the second was determined upon. Pages 1–46 of the second edition are printed from an entire resetting of type, while pages 47–[65] are printed from the same setting of type as

those pages in the first edition. These last-mentioned pages, however, are not a reissue of left-over sheets, but sheets newly impressed with a different ornament on page 64. Both Boston editions follow the text of the first London edition. The second Boston edition is not recorded in Evans's *American Bibliography*, and the only copy of it known to me is in the "Updike Pamphlets" in the Providence Public Library.

(4) The second London edition is not from the same sheets as the first, but seems to have been printed from an entire resetting of type with numerous minor revisions of text and typography. The text revisions are chiefly in modes of expression. I have not found the date of its publication but it does not seem to have come into the hands of the American booksellers until late in the year. In the *New York Mercury* of December 15, 1755, is an advertisement that reads: "From London just published . . . the second edition . . . the present state of North America."

(6) (7) (8) The easiest way to examine the German version of the *Present State* is to begin with No. 8. This work, the *Geographische und historisch-politsche Nachrichten* of 1756 is made up of two separate works bound together and provided with a general title and a "Nachricht des Herausgebers" in which it is explained that the two works, one representing the French side, the other the English, have been issued jointly so that readers might judge for themselves which of the two nations was in the right in the war just broken out. The two works are German translations of Butel-Dumont's *Histoire et Commerce des Colonies Angloises*, 1755, and (as first recognized in 1918 by Miss Alice H. Lerch and Mr. Leonard L. Mackall, then respectively of the New York Public Library and the Wymberley Jones De Renne Georgia Library) the greater part of Huske's *Present State of North America*, 1755. The German versions of these two books were first published separately in 1755. I have not found a copy of the Butel-Dumont translation, the *Geschichte und Handlung der Englischen Colonien*, bearing any other date than that of 1755, but the Huske translation, the *Allgemeine Amerikanische Kriegsgeschichte* of 1755 (copy in the New York Public Library) was reissued in 1756 with that date on the title-page. (See *Catalogue of the De Renne Georgia Library*, I, 136.) In putting the two works together under a general title in the order just named, the title-page of the *Geschichte und Handlung* was removed, but that of the *Allgemeine Amerikanische Kriegsgeschichte*,

bearing the date of the issue of 1756, was allowed to remain. The German version of the Butel-Dumont book is a full translation of the text of the French edition of 1755, the only difference I have found being the substitution of a *Vorbericht* entirely different from the original French *Avertissement*. The changes made in forming the German version of the Huske tract, on the other hand, are complex and extensive, and seem to have been based upon the German editor's feeling that Huske's presentation had been disorderly in its arrangement. The book contains pages xviii, 124. It is divided by the editor into six chapters instead of the three of the English original, and is made up as follows:

Title, as in No. 6 above; verso blank.

Vorbericht des Englischen Verfassers, pages III–VI.

The English edition of the book has no preface, but the German editor has translated the long note on page 4 of the original and placed it here as a *Vorbericht*, a purpose which, in ideas and phrasing, it admirably serves.

Einleitung, pages VII–XVIII

Comprises the general reflections found in the English original on pages 70–79, from paragraph, page 70, beginning "I say . . ." to paragraph, page 79, beginning "Thus much . . ."

Amerikanische Angelegenheiten zwischen Engeland und Frankreich, pages 1–96

This is the main text of the book, comprising a translation of pages 8–70 of the original English edition from paragraph, page 8, beginning "Acadie . . ." to paragraph, page 70, beginning "I say . . ."

Anhang, pages 97–108

Composed of two letters, the first, pages 97–103, dated at end "Paris, den 8. Aug. 1755," setting forth the French argument, and the second, pages 103–109, purporting to be a reply from someone in Brussels under date of August 18, in which the writer asserts that his Paris correspondent has not made out his case against the English. I have not been able to identify these letters as coming from a printed tract of the time. Their dates are useful in setting the period between August 18, 1755, and the end of that year as the time of publication of the German version of the Huske pamphlet.

Zugabe, pages 109–121

This section on the Newfoundland codfishery, attached to the

German version of the Huske pamphlet is a translation, surprisingly enough, of Butel-Dumont's *Histoire et Commerce*, Chapter II, Section II. It is, furthermore, a different translation to that which appears on pages 27–37 of the *Geschichte und Handlung der Englischen Colonien*, the version of Butel-Dumont's book with which the Huske book was later joined to form No. 8, above. This repetition of matter must mean that the two books were first conceived as entirely separate publications and that in the beginning there was no intention of ever issuing them together under a general title.

Neue Bücher, so zu Frankfurt und Leipzig Zu haben sind, pages 122–124

Map

"Karte von Canada und von dem Englishen Colonien am Ohio und St. Johan Fluss. I. M. Eben sc: Francofurti ad Moenum." A small, very rough map utterly unlike the Huske map, described below.

Plate [I]

Fischereij und . . . I. C. Back Sc. Title as in *De Renne Catalogue*, I, 136. An earlier version of this design, containing all its features, appears as an inset on the Herman Moll Map of North America, engraved by G. Vertue, and published, according to Phillips, *Maps of America*, page 566, in 1715. It is likely that the design was used in other works between 1715 and 1755, but I have not been able to find another example of its employment.

Plate [II]

Hinrichtung eines Kriegsgefangenē beij den Wilden.

I have not been able to identify this picture as used elsewhere.

Editor

The title-page of the *Allgemeine, etc.*, reads "und heraus gegeben von H.V.W." The "Nachricht des Herausgebers" of the joint book, the *Geographische, etc.*, is signed, "V.W." It is suggested in the *De Renne Catalogue* that these are the same, the H.V.W. meaning "Herr V.W." No one, however, has offered a suggestion as to the identity of this individual.

Additional notes

The German editor took extraordinary liberties with the construction of his English original in making up his new version, but somehow the book as rearranged by him seems more effective than in the English form. The omission of pages 79–88 of the original is understandable because those pages deal with fiscal matters and with details of the state of the two realms not particularly of interest to foreign readers. Pages 1–8 of the English original, to paragraph on page 8 beginning "Acadie . . .," are also omitted from the German version, probably because there is a certain amount of repetition of their matter elsewhere in the book.

A comparison shows that the German translation of this work above described was made from the text of the first English edition of the *Present State*.

The German editor has added a few notes. One of these, on pages 31 and 72, recommending those interested in the Indians to read Le Beau's *Avantures parmi les Sauvages de l'Amerique Septentrionale* (Field, *Essay*, No. 901) and citing a German translation of that book by J. B. Rack, is of doubtful value in view of the frequently questioned authenticity of Le Beau's narrative.

(9) *The Huske Map.* A note on the last page of the first London edition of the *Present State* reads: "N.B. The rest of this Work will be published with all possible Dispatch." On the last page of the second London edition, this note reads: "N.B. The rest of this Work will be published with all possible Dispatch, with an accurate Map of the Country, shewing the Rights of Great-Britain, France, and Spain." From this statement one may assume that the map was not issued with either the first or second London editions, though often, in later times, found with one or the other. But as it was announced to accompany Part II, never published, and as it follows from the sense of the note at the end of the second edition of Part I that it was issued after the publication of both editions of Part I, such copies of either edition of Part I as lack it cannot be said to be incomplete. Copies of this map are often found with Douglass's *Summary of the British Settlements in North America* in the edition of 1760; for example, in three copies in the New York Public Library, and in copies in the Library of Congress and the American Antiquarian Society, though Phillips, *Maps of America*, describes the Library of Congress copy as measuring only 16 x 14 inches instead of 15¾ x 19½ inches. Doubtless Dodsley, the publisher, found himself with a large edition of the Huske map left on his hands when Part II of the *Present State* failed to eventuate. Its appropriateness to the matter of Douglass's *Summary* determined its utilization as part of that book when Dodsley reprinted it five years later.

APPENDIX IV

[WILLIAM SMITH], A BRIEF
STATE OF THE PROVINCE
OF PENNSYLVANIA and
A BRIEF VIEW OF THE CONDUCT
OF PENNSYLVANIA

The full titles of these important and influential works and the several editions of the first of them are given by Wilberforce Eames in Sabin, Nos. 84589–84594. Under the first and last of these entries reasons are advanced for fixing the authorship of the two pamphlets upon William Smith. The suggestion sometimes made (see reference in Sabin, No. 84589) that the anonymous author had been assisted in the preparation of the *Brief State* by Benjamin Franklin seems to be without foundation. Though some of Franklin's ideas are found in the tract, it is most unlikely that the champion of the Assembly against the Proprietors could have had a hand in the writing of the most vigorous anti-Assembly document of the period and place. This tract was indeed, I believe, the beginning of the disagreement between Smith and Franklin that lasted so many years.

On August 27, 1756 (Smyth, *Writings of Benjamin Franklin*, III, 276), Franklin wrote as follows to Peter Collinson: "I believe I have already wrote you, that our Friend Smith is not thought here to be the Author of the Pamphlet you mention. 'Tis generally suppos'd to be the Governor's (with some Help from one or two others) as his Messages are fill'd with the same sentiments and almost the same Expressions. He is, I think, the rashest and most indiscreet Governor that I have known, . . ." That Franklin came to hold another belief as to the authorship of the pamphlet is clear from a letter to Isaac Norris of June 9, 1759 (Mason Library, No. 223, unpublished, but quoted from copiously by George Simpson Eddy in "Account Book of Benjamin Franklin, 1757–1762," *Pennsylvania Magazine of History and Biography*, LV, No. 2, 1931, page 121), in which, discussing the *Historical Review of the Government of Pennsylvania*, lately published, Franklin wrote: "It is also a full refutation of Smith's Brief States and Brief View, without doing the author the honour of taking the least notice of him or his work."

On December 24, 1754, Governor Morris wrote as follows (*Pennsylvania Archives*, II, 225) to Thomas Penn: "I send you herewith a state of the Province of Pensilvania Put in my hands a few days ago, and I find is Intended for the Press in England, In order to Induce the Parliament to take measures for the future security of this Province, by Excluding the Quakers from the Legislature. Those who knew the affairs of the Country say it is well drawn up, But that you will judge of, being better acquainted wth the severall matters set forth in it than any body Elce. The Persons Concern'd in this state are very much your friends, and as they Insist upon taking this measure I thought it Proper you should Know it, and have a Coppy of what was Intended for the Press."

It is clear from Governor Morris's statement that the tract was written in Pennsylvania. In its text, page 24, a reference to an incident in the Assembly's Indian relations indicates that the piece was still in process of composition in the early part of December, 1754. It seems clear from the sentences quoted below that the Proprietor was not given the opportunity to edit the work before publication. In a letter to Governor Morris of February 26, 1755 (*Pennsylvania Archives*, II, 257–258), he wrote: "I had some of the pamphlets sent me this day, and think with regard to the Quakers and Assembly what is said is propper enough, but I think a representation to the king, or some of these printed to give away to leading men would have been better, than to publish them to the world, and cannot have any good effect; the appealing to a Parliament is no compliment to an administration, and even therefore when they agree so well as at this time, will not be found a proper manner of applying to get the business done, however they will soon find whether it will answer their purpose. I have now again mentioned the impossibility of getting any thing done for the defence of the Country, while people are allowed to sit in the House that scruple to bear arms, but there is very little said to it, from whence I judge it will be difficult to bring about a change, but if such a thing was proposed in a representation from People of the Country, some answer would be given to it. I think the language of the pamphlet too violent, however, I shall hear what others say of any consequence, and then write you further."

The pamphlets received by Mr. Penn on February 26, 1755, may have been advance copies, but publication was certainly not long delayed. The *Gentleman's Magazine* for March, 1755, page 140, lists it among books published in March. It was reviewed fully in the *Monthly Review* for March, 1755, pages 191–199, by Ralph Griffiths, editor and publisher of that periodical (Information from Benjamin C. Nangle of Yale University), who begins: "The facts contained in this pamphlet appear to be (at this juncture) of such importance to the public, and the authority from whence they come, is said to be so considerable, that we judge it very proper to lay some extracts of the most interesting passages before our readers." The extracts then given comprise a large part of the pamphlet. This same writer reviewed the *Brief View of the Conduct of Pennsylvania*, London, 1756, in his periodical for March, 1756, giving fifteen pages (208–223) of his space to the publication in which Dr. Smith replied to his critics and pointed to Braddock's defeat and the Indian invasion as the logical consequence of the influence of the Quaker in the Pennsylvania Assembly. It is interesting to observe that the effect of these pamphlets upon Griffiths was modified very much by the other side of the case represented in Charles Thomson's *Enquiry into the Alienation of the Indians*. See the discussion of that work in the foregoing text.

APPENDIX V

[JOSEPH GALLOWAY], A TRUE AND IMPARTIAL STATE OF PENNSYLVANIA

1. A True and Impartial State Of the Province of Pennsylvania. . . .
The whole being a full Answer to the Pamphlets intitled A Brief
State, and A Brief View, &c. of the Conduct of Pennsylvania. . . .
Philadelphia: Printed by W. Dunlap, at the Newest-Printing-Office,
M,DCC,LIX.

> 8vo. [I–II], i–v, [vi], 3–80, 79–173, [174], 1–34, [35]. Page
> [I]: title, verso blank; pages i–v: [Dedication] "To the Right
> Honorable William Pitt, Esq; . . ."; pages 3–80, 79–173: "A
> True and Impartial State, &c."; pages 1–34: "An Appendix. To
> the Foregoing Work. Copy of the Eleventh Article of the Pro-
> prietary Instructions."; page [35]: "Advertisement."

The determination of authorship of this book has had a strange
history. Horace Wemyss Smith in a moment of inexplicable thought-
lessness included it among the works of Dr. William Smith (*Life*,
II, 535), when a glance at its title should have told him that it had
been written in indignant reply to Dr. Smith's *Brief State* and *Brief
View*. Charles R. Hildeburn's *Issues of the Press in Pennsylvania*,
No. 1649, calls attention to this error, and then suggests that the
tract was inspired, if not wholly written, by Franklin. This attribution was accepted tentatively by Ford, *Franklin Bibliography*, No.
261, on Hildeburn's authority. Evans, No. 8349, enters it as by
Franklin, but queries the attribution. Various considerations—style;
Franklin's interest in the preparation in England of the *Historical
Review of the Government of Pennsylvania*, a book of similar tenor,
at the same time that this tract was being written in America; the
publication of this book in Philadelphia when the other Pennsylvania pieces in which he was interested in these years were published
under his eye in London—combine to lead one to doubt the attribution of the tract to him. That this doubt is solidly based appears
from the reply to an inquiry I addressed to Mr. George Simpson
Eddy of New York, whose extended, diligent, and revealing re-

searches have brought to light so much of interest in Franklin's life and work. In a letter of April 24, 1933, Mr. Eddy was able to answer my inquiry in the following satisfactory fashion: "A True and Impartial State of the Province of Pennsylvania . . . was written by Joseph Galloway, as appears from a letter to Galloway, written by William Franklin, London, Dec. 28, 1759, in which William Franklin says:

> It gives me great Pleasure to hear that your Answer to the Brief State has exceeded your Expectations, and has tended so much to open the Eyes of the People of the neighbouring Colonies. We did not receive one of them from you or any other of our friends in Pensylvania. However we met with some at a Bookseller's in London, to whom Mr. Dunlap had sent a Number for Sale. Several of my Acquaintance, upon my Recommendation, have purchased them, and have since expressed their Approbation of the Performance. It has informed them of several important Facts which they were not so well acquainted with before. I have also desired the Bookseller to advertise them again this Winter, while the Company are in Town, and make no doubt but they will all be sold.

The letter in question, unpublished, is owned by Mr. William Smith Mason."

The extract quoted above from William Franklin's letter to Joseph Galloway is printed here through the courteous permission of its owner, Mr. William Smith Mason, of Evanston, Illinois.

The advertising of *A True and Impartial State* in the *Newport Mercury* for several issues beginning with that of July 3, 1759, seems to indicate a determination on the part of those behind the book to inform the other colonies of the causes responsible for Pennsylvania's lack of vigor in the prosecution of the war.

APPENDIX VI

THE MAPS AND GEOGRAPHICAL
ESSAYS OF LEWIS EVANS

1. A Map of Pensilvania, New-Jersey, New-York, and the Three Delaware Counties: By Lewis Evans. MDCCXLIX. Published by Lewis Evans March 25 1749 according to Act of Parliament. L. Hebert Sculp^t. [Philadelphia.] [Benjamin Franklin?]

2. *Title as in No. 1.* The Second Edition. July, 1752.

   For full description and facsimiles of both issues in ¾ scale see Henry N. Stevens, *Lewis Evans*, 1924, and for discussion, see below under *The Map of 1749.*

3. A general Map of the Middle British Colonies, in America; . . . By Lewis Evans. 1755. Engraved by Ja^s Turner in Philadelphia. Published according to Act of Parliament, by Lewis Evans, June 23. 1755. and sold by R. Dodsley, in Pall-Mall, London, & by the Author in Philadelphia.

   For full description and ¾ scale facsimile, see work cited under No. 2, above, in which are also found titles, descriptions, and comparisons of eighteen editions, issues, variants, and copies between 1755 and 1814. For discussion containing supplementary information, see below under *The Map of 1755.*

4. Geographical, Historical, Political, Philosophical and Mechanical Essays. The First, containing An Analysis Of a General Map of the Middle British Colonies In America; . . . By Lewis Evans. Philadelphia: Printed by B. Franklin, and D. Hall. MDCCLV.

   4to. Pages i–iv, 1–32.

   For full title and collation, see Campbell, *Collection of Franklin Imprints*, page 125. For further discussion, see section below, THE "GEOGRAPHICAL ESSAYS."

5. *Title as in No. 4.* Printed by B. Franklin, and D. Hall. MDCCLV. And sold by R. and J. Dodsley, in Pall-Mall, London.

   See work cited in No. 4, above, pages 125–126.

6. *Title as in No. 4.* The Second Edition. Philadelphia: Printed by B. Franklin, and D. Hall. MDCCLV.

   See work cited in No. 4, above, page 126. This is a complete resetting of type throughout.

7. *Title as in No. 4.* The Second Edition. Philadelphia: Printed by B. Franklin, and D. Hall. MDCCLV. And sold by J. and R. Dodsley, in Pall-Mall, London.

See work cited in No. 4, above, page 126.

8. Geographical, Historical, Political, Philosophical and Mechanical Essays. Number II. Containing, A Letter Representing, the Impropriety of sending Forces to Virginia: . . . Published in the New-York Mercury, No. 178, Jan. 5. 1756. With An Answer, To so much thereof as concerns the Public; . . . By Lewis Evans. Philadelphia: Printed for the Author [by B. Franklin and D. Hall]; and Sold by him in Arch-Street: And at New-York by G. Noel, Bookseller near Counts's Market. MDCCLVI.

4to. Pages 1–43.

For full title and collation, see work cited in No. 4, above, page 130. For a discussion, see below under section headed THE "GEOGRAPHICAL ESSAYS."

9. Geographical, Historical, Political, Philosophical, and Mechanical Essays. No. II. By Lewis Evans. Dodsley.

4to. Page 35.

I have not seen a copy of this separately printed English edition of *Geographical Essays, No. II.* The title is taken from the *Monthly Review*, September, 1756, page 312, and the collation from Stevens, *Lewis Evans*, 1924, page 14. A full title is given in the *Rare Americana* catalogue, No. 5 (1933), of Henry Stevens, Son and Stiles, item 110.

GENERAL STATEMENT

The chief source of knowledge of the Evans maps and the *Geographical Essays*, [No. I] and No. II, is Henry N. Stevens, *Lewis Evans his Map of the Middle British Colonies in America, etc.* Third Edition, London, 1924. (First edition, 1905; second, 1920.) With his notable faculty for close observation in the making of cartographical comparisons, Mr. Stevens gave in this work an impressive statement of the history and influence of the Evans maps, especially of the map of 1755. As his treatment of the subject was chiefly cartographical, it seems to me desirable to record here some additional information about a series of works hardly excelled in interest and importance by any product of the colonial American press.

It is generally said that Lewis Evans was a native Pennsylvanian, born about the year 1700, whose occupation was that of a land surveyor. In the Preface to Bartram's *Observations in his Travels to Lake Ontario,*

London, 1751, he is described as "a skilfull surgeon," but as no other references to Evans as a surgeon have been found, one may suggest that a hurried compositor could easily have misread the word "surveyor" for "surgeon" in the editor's manuscript. After a life of great activity in travel, surveying, writing, map-making, and scientific investigation, Evans died on June 12, 1756, under circumstances that will be related in course. On September 9, 1756, "John Evans, Executor" advertised in the *Pennsylvania Gazette* that all demands against the estate of Lewis Evans should be presented and all indebtedness to it paid. In the Du Simitière Collection in the Library Company of Philadelphia is an unpublished manuscript of 23 pages measuring approximately 15 × 9 inches entitled *A Brief Account of Pennsylvania in a Letter to Richard Peters, Esqʳ. in answer to some Queries of a Gentleman in Europe, by Lewis Evans MDCCLIII.* The manuscript is a copy, probably in Du Simitière's hand and with Du Simitière's notes, of an admirable description of many important features of the Province. The following extract from its preface is of special interest:

> As the answer to the foregoing Queries, was not intended for the publick, the writer designedly dwells on the more popular matters, and omitt[s] many others that he might have added to render the several articles complete, lest the Publication of this should anticipate him in a design he has entertain'd, of troubling the publick one day, with a natural, artificial, Civil, & Political History, of this & some of the neighbouring Colonies.

One regrets that the author lived to carry out only a small part of this intention in the form of the Map of 1755 and the *Geographical Essays* of that year, described below.

THE MAP OF 1749

The publication of Evans's Map of 1749 and its reissue with corrections in 1752 seem to have been accomplished by Evans upon his own initiative, with only slight aid from the government. The journey he undertook to Lake Ontario with John Bartram and Conrad Weiser in 1743, the route of which is recorded on the map of 1749, and an account of which by him is found in Appendix V of Thomas Pownall's *Topographical Description*, 1776, undoubtedly added much to his knowledge of the western country, and may even have been the origin of his later topographical studies and maps. It is probable that he began working upon the Map of 1749 soon after this experience. In an undated letter, ascribed to the autumn of 1745 (*Colden Papers*, III, 180), John Bartram speaks of Evans being under obligation to Cadwallader Colden. This may have been the same obligation that Evans later acknowledged on the face of the Map of 1749 in the words: "And the greatest Part of New York Province is owing to the honourable Cadwallader Colden, Esqr." But whether or not the association between Evans and Colden had been brought about thus early in the preparation of the map, it is certain that Colden's aid became important to the cartographer as the work upon it progressed. The following letter from Evans to Colden, dated Philadelphia, March 13, 1748/49 (*Colden Papers*, IV, 107–108), makes that point clear:

> My very worthy Friend
>
> My Map is finisht at last, & now waits upon you for your Amendment, which if you could favour me with by the first Opportunity w^d oblige me much; for I wait now but for Mr Alexander's & your Revisal, before I proceed to print them off, & get them ready for Publication.
>
> I sh^d be glad you would minute down some more Variations; how far the Settlements extend back because I intend to colour so far; Addition of Towns, noted Houses, Roads & intermediate Distances of Places &c. & these I w^d get incerted on the Plate before Printing off. Please to mark them with red Ink if you have any by you.
>
> There come also some Specimens with Receipts to the Amount of 70 Pieces of Eight, that you may perhaps prevail on Somebody your Way to dispose of.
>
> This has happened unluckily y^t I had ne'er a Copy to Send you but this, that has been so much handled & dirty'd.
>
> I am Sir with greatest Respects to y^r Self and Family, of whose Welfare I always rejoyce to hear. Y^r most obliged humble serv^t
>
> Lewis Evans

From the sense of this letter and from other circumstances one assumes that the copy of the map sent to Colden was one of a number of preliminary specimen copies known to have been printed about this time. Newspaper advertisements of this winter and spring, specifically one in the *Pennsylvania Gazette* for February 28, 1748/49, announced that the plate was completed and that a few sample copies printed from it were to be seen at the subscription agencies. On May 1, the *New York Post-Boy* carried a letter from a disgruntled resident of Orange County, New York, accusing Evans of having been bribed by the Jersey proprietors to run his New York–New Jersey boundary in such fashion as to cut off many square miles of New York territory. In his reply dated "Philadelphia May 11, 1749" (*New York Post-Boy*, May 15, 1749), Evans asserted his willingness to make a change if convinced that his running of the line was incorrect, but challenged his critic to produce acceptable evidence that this was the case. This anonymous critic must have acquired his knowledge of the map from one of the specimen copies on view at Mr. Parker's New York printing office, for though the map as issued bore the date March 25, 1749, it was not until the 24th of July that it was given general distribution, if we may believe the announcement to that effect in the *Pennsylvania Gazette* for July 13, 1749. In the same newspaper for August 3, 1749, the map was for the first time advertised as "just published."

PLACE OF PUBLICATION

Writers upon the subject of the map of 1749 have been chary of expressing themselves as to its place of publication. The map is not recorded by Sabin, nor does Hildeburn include it in his *Issues of the Press in Pennsylvania*. Stevens does not give special consideration to the point. Phillips, *Maps of America*, page 571, gave its place of publication as Philadelphia, but confusion entered the record when Charles Evans, *American Bibliography*, No. 6316, listed it without qualification as a publication of the New York press of James Parker. It is probable that the frequent mention of the map in Parker's *New York Post-Boy* provided the basis for this attribution, though it seems clear that such of these references as point to any specific place of publication point to Philadelphia and not to New York. In his note to this entry, Mr. Evans seems also to believe, incorrectly, that the map of 1749 was an early issue of the map of 1755, and to assume that its publication in the earlier year did not meet with success. In the paragraphs that follow will be given the evidence for the acceptance of Philadelphia as the place of publication of the map.

(a) Under date of October 13, 1748 (for these references to James Parker's *New York Post-Boy* I am indebted to Stokes, *Iconography of Manhattan Island*, IV, 614–615), the Philadelphia correspondence in the *New York Post-Boy* for October 17th referred to the map that Lewis Evans prepared and had "engrav'd by a good Artist, under his Eye." Under date of February 27, 1748/49, a note in the *Post-Boy* read: "We hear from Philadelphia, that the Map of these Provinces by Mr. Evans is now compleated, and hope in a Week or two an account of the Publication of it." In the *Pennsylvania Gazette* for October 13,

1748, the date of the Philadelphia item in the *New York Post-Boy* referred to above, another news item announced that "The map of Pennsylvania, New-Jersey and New York Provinces, by Mr. Lewis Evans, is now engraving here, and in great Forwardness . . . is having his map engrav'd by a good Artist, under his eye." It seems that the sense of these quotations joined to the fact that it was from Philadelphia that Evans wrote to Colden, "My Map is finisht at last," combine to point to Philadelphia rather than to New York as the place of publication of the map of 1749. This conclusion is supported by other circumstances attendant upon the publication of the map, for example:

(b) On August 19, 1749, an entry in the *Votes and Proceedings of the Pennsylvania Assembly* (Miller ed., IV, 114–115) records that

Lewis Evans having presented this House with a Map done by him, of this and the neighboring Provinces, Ordered, that a Present be made him from this House of Ten Pounds, in Reward of his Industry and Ingenuity in making the said Map.

And an Order was accordingly drawn on the Treasurer for Payment of the same, and signed by the Speaker.

Under the incidental charges in the public accounts of this session is the entry: "To Lewis Evans, a Present from the House £ 10 – 0 – 0."

(c) The presence in 1749 of an engraver named L. Hebert or Herbert (see section below, The Engraver) is not recorded, so far as is known, in any American city except Philadelphia.

(d) Finally, the argument for Philadelphia as the place of publication seems to be clinched by certain words of Thomas Pownall's in his *Topographical Description*, 1776, page 45: "I cannot close these Observations," he writes, "without transcribing from Lewis Evans's Map of Pennsylvania, New York, and New Jersey, printed at Philadelphia 1749, the following . . ." It might be objected that after a lapse of twenty-seven years, Pownall's memory could well have been at fault, but taken in connection with the evidence accumulated in the foregoing paragraph, one is inclined to allow full value to his statement that Philadelphia was the place of publication of the map of 1749. I have not found definite evidence that Franklin was its printer, but in the "just published" announcement in the *Pennsylvania Gazette* of August 3, 1749, it is said that the map is "to be sold at the Post-Office and by the author, in Philadelphia." Furthermore in advertisements in the same paper on September 12, October 10 and 17, 1754, it is said that a few copies of the map may still be secured from "the Author in Arch-street, at the New-Printing Office, in Market-street, Philadelphia, and at Mr.

James Parker's, at the New-Printing-Office, in Beaver street, New York." The naming of the "Post-Office" and the "New-Printing Office," Philadelphia, in these advertisements seems to associate the map with Franklin, the acknowledged publisher of the later Evans map of 1755.

THE ENGRAVER

The engraver's name is signed in the lower right-hand corner of the map: "L. Hebert Sculp^t." Neither D. McN. Stauffer in his *American Engravers upon Copper and Steel* (Grolier Club, 1907) nor A. C. Prime in his *Arts and Crafts in Philadelphia, Maryland and South Carolina* (Walpole Society, 1929) records an engraver of this name, but both these authorities list the name of "Lawrence Herbert" as an engraver of Philadelphia. Stauffer refers to the advertisements of "Lawrence Herbert" in the *Pennsylvania Gazette* for October 16, 1748, and August 1, 1751, but as there seems to have been no *Gazette* published on October 16, that particular reference is not very helpful. It becomes even less helpful in determining the correct form of the name when we find by recourse to the original that in the other advertisement Mr. Stauffer refers to, that of August 1, 1751, the name of the engraver is printed as "Lawrence Hebert." Mr. Prime quotes correctly from the *Pennsylvania Gazette* of May 19, 1748, the advertisement of an engraver "Lawrence Herbert." Identity of place of residence, identity of occupation, nearness in dates of employment, and close similarity in Christian name and surname leave us little reason to doubt that these three forms of name represent the same individual, but it still remains to determine which of these is the correct form.

To summarize the existing knowledge on this point, we record here these three contemporary uses of the name:

Pennsylvania Gazette, May 19, 1748—Lawrence Herbert
Evans Map of 1749, March, 1749—L. Hebert Sculp^t
Pennsylvania Gazette, August 1, 1751—Lawrence Hebert

Of these three uses of the name two are in the "Hebert" form, and of these two, one was engraved upon a copper plate by the engraver himself or under his direction. Under these circumstances, one is inclined to regard "Hebert" as the correct form of name of the man who engraved the Evans map of 1749.

OTHER ISSUES

I have not learned of any issue of the map bearing the name of a London publisher, but we learn that it attained a certain degree of foreign circulation from the concluding sentences of the Preface of John Bartram's *Observations* of London, 1751. "I shall only add," writes the editor, "that Mr. Lewis Evans a companion of our author's in this journey, and a skilful surgeon, has lately publish'd a map of New York, Pensilvania, and Jersey, with part of Virginia, Maryland and New-England, chiefly founded on actual surveys. This map includes the route here described, which seems laid down very exactly. And is sold by Mr. Bowle's [*sic*] map and print-seller in Cornhill."

In the summer of 1923, Henry N. Stevens discovered in Boston a copy of the second issue of the map of 1749, dated July, 1752, the only copy of that issue yet discovered, though its existence, predicated upon a statement in Evans's *Geographical Essays* and upon newspaper advertisements of 1752–1754, had previously been known. Mr. Stevens's elation at this discovery (how well many of us remember his telling of it!) led him to bring out in 1924, a third edition of his *Lewis Evans*. In that book (pages 1–4 immediately after the title), are fully described by the enthusiastic student of cartography the several corrections and additions made to the original issue of 1749 in the issue of 1752. I have not found advertisements indicating the publication of the issue of 1752 as early as July of that year, the date which appears upon its face, but for two years afterwards it continued occasionally to be offered for sale in the *Pennsylvania Gazette* and the *New York Post-Boy*. The creation of new counties in Pennsylvania, the correction of errors, and, above all, the decree in Chancery of May 15, 1750, fixing the Maryland-Pennsylvania boundary at 39° 44' were the motives underlying the new issue of the map. On February 25, 1751, Thomas Penn had written Governor Hamilton (Boyd, *The Susquehannah Company Papers*, I, 8): "The North Boundary must be carried higher than Evans has done it in his Map, so as to take three Degrees from the line of the Agreement with Maryland which will carry it almost as high as the head of Sasquehanna River by Evans's Map . . ." In the revised map Evans suggested 42° 44' as the northern boundary of Pennsylvania, saying that the Royal Patent and the recent decree in Chancery would "probably" run Mr. Penn's limits to that point, but it is to be observed that he did not erase the old inscription along the 42d parallel, which read "The Bounds of Pensilvania by Patent."

THE MAP OF 1755

As related in the text, Lewis Evans was engaged June 26, 1750, by the Council of Pennsylvania to spy out the western bounds of the colony. The agreement then made is of particular interest in colonial political history, keeping in mind intercolonial jealousies in the matter of chartered boundaries, especially the disagreement between Pennsylvania and Virginia as to their respective western limits. For the full text of this agreement, the reader is referred to the *Pennsylvania Archives*, II, 47–49. For reasons that will appear it is of interest to remark at this point that in that agreement Evans was enjoined, by implication certainly, to learn the limits of Lord Fairfax's Virginia grants as determined by the relative western position of the north and south forks of the Potomac, and that he was urged if possible to extend his observations to the shores of Lake Erie.

It must be admitted that, though of importance in the study of intercolonial relations in this period, the agreement cited above loses some of its force as a document in the study of Lewis Evans and his maps when a doubt arises, and must be expressed, as to whether Evans actually went upon the mission projected in the agreement. The date of the agreement was June 26, 1750. On June 28th, Franklin wrote to Cadwallader Colden: ". . . Mr. Evans is about to take a Journey to Lake Erie, which he intends next Week." (*Colden Papers*, IV, 219.) On February 14, 1750/51, the Governor of Pennsylvania wrote to the Board of Trade (*Pennsylvania Archives*, II, 60–63) that when he had received their queries of July 19, [1750], he had not been able to reply to them because he lacked at that time a good map of the Province and that the person needed to make such a map was then at "a great distance in the uncultivated Parts of the Province." He enclosed with this letter of February 14th, however, a map that one assumes he had lately acquired. Franklin's statement and the inference to be derived from the Governor's letter lead one to suppose that Evans had gone upon the trip as planned, but to offset this assumption is another letter from Franklin to Colden dated October 11th, 1750, in which he says: "Mess.ᵣˢ Bertram and Evans did not go their intended Journey to Lake Erie but are both safe at home." (*Colden Papers*, IV, 227.) One turns to the *Geographical Essays*, in which Evans gives his sources for the information embodied in his map of 1755, especially to page 24, in which he discusses, apparently not at first hand, the question as to whether the "North Branch or the South Branch of the Potomac was the farther West." He had been particularly charged in the agreement of June 26th to examine this question in the course of his journey, and if he had made the journey and had been enabled to follow his instructions in this particular he would probably have given his opinion from his own observations, just as he did in other instances in which information had been acquired by his personal surveys or computations. In the same book in discussing the neighborhood of Lake Erie he does not give any indication of personal knowledge of that part of the country. Turning to the public accounts of 1751 (*V & P of the Pennsylvania Assembly,* Miller ed. IV, 197–201) we find that there is no reference to a payment of 100 guineas to Lewis Evans, and it is in this statement that the payment would normally have been entered if the project had been carried out. In the earlier public accounts for 1750, however, dated August 18th of that year (*ibid.,* IV, 148) there is an entry of a payment to Lewis Evans, service not specified, of £10–0–0. If the journey to the westward had been called off, the sum mentioned might have been paid in reimbursement of expenses undergone by him in preparation for it. It may be remarked that in the second, or 1752, issue of his map of 1749 there is no evidence that Evans had acquired new information of the western boundaries of Pennsylvania, Maryland, and Virginia, though he embodies in it changes relating to the eastern section of those colonies.

But regardless of whether he went upon the journey, the West had taken hold upon Evans's mind. Though we find him in New York in July, 1751, lecturing upon natural philosophy and mechanics, including recent discoveries in electricity (Stokes, *Iconography of Manhattan Island,* IV, 628), and a longer search might show him busy in these years at his profession of surveying, it is probable that he began about this time collecting the materials for his map and book of 1755. On October 16th, 1754, he asked aid for such a project from the Pennsylvania Assembly in the following terms (*V & P of the Pennsylvania Assembly,* Miller ed. IV, 330, 334):

A Petition from Lewis Evans, of the City of Philadelphia, was presented to the House and read, setting forth, that the Petitioner hath, with much Labour and Expence, prepared Materials for a Map of this and four of the neighbouring Colonies; the Country of the Six Nations from Lake Champlain, its North-Eastern Extremity, to the Falls of Ohio; the Lakes Champlain, Ontario and Erie; the Routes from Albany to Oswego, and, by Crown Point, to Canada (the latter being the Pass that the French and Indians harrass the Governments of New-York and New-England by;) the Routes from Canada to Yawgra, Ohio and Detroit, and by the Outawas River, and the Lake Huron to Detroit (being for the greatest Part their usual Way to the Western Nations;) and the Connection and Situation of the English and French Colonies with the Land of the Six Nations, the undoubted Property of the King of Great-Britain, a Country equal in Magnitude to all the Plantations yet made by the English on this Continent: That the Petitioner is unable to support the Expence of Engraving and Printing the said Map, and of printing an Analysis containing his Authority for every Part thereof, as well as a Description of all the remoter Parts, and the Manner of Travelling from Place to Place through Countries destitute of common Roads; the Petitioner therefore prays that this House would grant him such Assistance in the Premises as to their Wisdom shall seem meet. Ordered to lie on the Table.

On October 19th:

The Petition from Lewis Evans was again read, and considered; and, after some Time spent therein, it was

Resolved, That the Sum of Fifty Pounds be paid out of the Provincial Treasury to the said Evans, towards the better enabling him to compleat and publish the Map mentioned in his said Petition.

And an Order was accordingly drawn on the Treasurer, and signed by the Speaker, by Order of the House, for Payment of the same.

In the statement of Public Accounts for the period October 14, 1754, to September 30, 1755 (*V & P of the Pennsylvania Assembly*, Miller ed. IV, 481), occurs this entry: "For Lewis Evans, towards his Map of this and the adjacent Provinces £ 50–0–0." In the opening paragraph of the introduction to his *Geographical Essays* [No. I], Evans makes acknowledgment of the aid thus accorded him by the Assembly.

The next information we have showing the progress of the work is drawn from the definite assertion by Evans in his *Geographical Essays*, No. II, Philadelphia, 1756, page 25. "My Map," he writes, "was begun engraving in November 1754, and finished towards the end of June 1755. The Pamphlet published August 9, next following."

On July 10, 1755, the *Pennsylvania Gazette* announced that "Mr. Evans's Map of the Middle British Colonies . . . is just finished engraving, and next Saturday Proposals for publishing the same by subscription will be given gratis at the Printers hereof." (No copy of these separately printed Proposals seems to have been recorded by bibliographers.) On July 17, these proposals were published in the *Gazette* with the additional statement that specimen copies had been printed off. The map was to be delivered when 500 subscriptions had been secured. On July 24, 1755, the *Gazette* advertised, "This Day is published a General Map . . . by Lewis Evans." Thereafter the advertisements concerning it are found frequently in the newspapers of Philadelphia, New York, and Boston. For example, on August 11 proposals were published in the *Boston Evening Post*, saying that a few sample maps are finished and one may be examined at the printer's. In all these advertisements Evans lays emphasis upon the map saying that subscribers to the colored copies of the map will receive the pamphlet describing it free. He also asserts that the pamphlet will be sold separately, and though the pamphlet was written very largely as a guide to the map, or an "Analysis" of it, as he calls it, yet many copies must have been sold without the map, and many copies of the map without the book. The American Antiquarian Society, for example, possesses a copy of the map that has never been folded. In view of these circumstances it may be incorrect to say that the pamphlet, that is, the book we know as *Geographical Essays*, is incomplete without the map, though it seems that a colored copy of the map is not a true collector's piece unless it is accompanied by the pamphlet that was given free with it. The John Carter Brown colored copy of the map is bound in a contemporary binding with a copy of the book which proclaims itself in a fine clear inscription on a fly-leaf to have been presented to John Pownall, Secretary to the Board of Trade, by his "most obedient and most humble Servt. Lewis Evans."

It was some weeks after the publication of the proposals for subscription that the maps and books were delivered in New York and more distant cities. The *Pennsylvania Gazette* announced the map promptly enough as "published" on July 24, 1755. The *New York Post-Boy* and the *New York Mercury* did not make a similar announcement until August 25 and September 1, respectively; and it was not until October 23 that the *Boston Weekly News-Letter* advertised that a number of the maps "are come hither from Philadelphia" and are ready for subscribers. Evans's Map of 1755 and the *Geographical Essays* were advertised frequently in this year throughout the Middle Colonies and New England. Few colonial publications were given so great a degree of publicity as these.

BRADDOCK AND THE MAP OF 1755

It is of some interest to examine the statement often made that the Evans map of 1755 was used by Braddock in his Monongahela campaign. Evans asserted that its engraving was completed towards the end of June, 1755, and the map itself bears the statement that it was "Published according to Act of Parliament June 23, 1755." On July 3, 1755 (*Pennsylvania Archives*, II, 373), Governor Morris wrote to Braddock that, in order that the General might know where the new road across Pennsylvania would meet his own route, "I send you herewith Evans's map, now publishing, which is not yet complete, that it might be useful to you. I got this sheet printed off on purpose." Six days later, certainly before the messenger could have reached the Monongahela, the fatal defeat had occurred and Braddock was dying.

This does not mean, however, that the tradition is without foundation. As early as February 28, 1755 (*Minutes of Provincial Council,* VI, 301–302), Governor Morris had written to Sir John St. Clair, then about to join Braddock, that he had prevailed upon one Evans to let him have for his use "a Map of the back country from the Materials he has in his Hands . . . and from the best Information I can get and in the Judgement of those here most acquainted with that Country it is more to be depended upon than any other." One suggests that this "Map of the back country" was a manuscript sectional map and not the larger work as afterwards published. Again on May 12, 1755, Richard Peters wrote William Shirley, Braddock's aide, that he was sending enclosed Mr. Evans's map. (*Pennsylvania Archives,* II, 309.) This was nearly two months before the letter of July 3rd in which Governor Morris described the engraved map as "not yet complete." The copy sent young Shirley may have been an engraver's proof. Shirley acknowledged the map, sent some subscriptions to it and said that he would try to get more at a later time. (*Pennsylvania Archives,* II, 317.) It may be that through St. Clair and Shirley, Braddock was assisted to some extent by Evans's map, and though one would suppose that a large-area, small-scale map such as this, even when complete, could only have been of aid to a military commander in the most general way, yet Thomas Pownall is emphatic upon the point that the map was very useful to the armies in their western campaigns. (*Topographical Description,* page iv.)

THE "GEOGRAPHICAL ESSAYS"

Geographical Essays [No. 1] has been discussed fully in the foregoing text. The following bibliographical note is from Stevens's *Lewis Evans,* 3d ed. pages 5–6:

This *Analysis,* which accompanied the Map, was issued in the form of a closely printed quarto pamphlet (iv + 32pp.). It was printed by B. Franklin and D. Hall at Philadelphia in 1755, and two editions appeared the same year. The fact that they are distinct impressions throughout shows that there must have been sufficient demand for the work to have exhausted the first edition and made a reprint necessary. As the two editions are very similar in appearance, it is more than likely the second was printed from standing type corrected; but there are sufficient differences on every page to clearly indicate the entire reimpression. The second edition may readily be detected by the printers' mark on the first and third pages of each sheet, viz., a small figure 2 beneath the last line of text (but above the footnotes), half an inch in from the left margin. This mark is found on pages 1, 3, 9, 11, 17, 19, 25, and 27. More or less alteration has been made on every page, but the following will serve for easy identification. The first edition has no sectional headings on pages 6 and 11, whereas in the second headings have been inserted, *The Face of the Country* on page 6 between lines 7 and 8, and *The Boundaries of the Confederates, &c.* on page 11 in the centre.

It was probably due to the suggestion of Thomas Pownall (to whom the Map is dedicated, and who was in Philadelphia at the time of publication), that some copies of the Map and the *Analysis* were also prepared for the English market, for certain copies of both the First and Second Editions bear the additional line in the imprint, "and sold by J. & R. Dodsley in Pall-Mall, London." There are therefore four distinct issues of the title-page of the *Analysis*, viz., the First and Second Editions with the imprint of B. Franklin and D. Hall alone, and the First and Second Editions with the additional Dodsley imprint. There do not appear to be any other variations between the Philadelphia and London issues of either edition.

The occasion for the writing of *Geographical Essays, No. II*, was the attack upon certain of Evans's ideas that appeared in the form of a letter, dated December 1, 1755, in the *New York Mercury* for January 5, 1756. Evans set to work at once upon his reply to this letter and seems to have been most diligent in his efforts, for the date at the end of its main portion is January 10, 1756. This does not mean, however, as sometimes asserted, that the book was published immediately after this date. It carries, indeed, a "Postscript" dated at the end March 1, 1756, and it was not until March 25, 1756, that it was announced as "just published" in the *Pennsylvania Gazette*. In the note referred to below from his *History of New-York*, William Smith, Jr. says that the book was published in the spring of 1756. A second letter of the same tenor, dated January 26, 1756, appeared in the *New York Mercury* for February 2, but though there was plenty of time to take that letter also into consideration, Evans seems to have disregarded it in his reply. It has been suggested in the foregoing text that the *Mercury* letters emanated from the Smith-Livingston-Alexander group. The *Monthly Review* for September, 1756, page 312, after speaking of the *Geographical Essays*

[No. I] as an "ingenious, public-spirited, and useful work," said of Evans's defense of himself in No. II against the *Mercury* attack that "our Author replies, with the appearance of much solidity of argument, as well as honesty of intention. He was, certainly, a sensible man, a good geographer, (so far, at least, as concerns that part of the world he treats of) and a true friend to his country; so that his death may justly be deemed a public loss." Evans succeeded, indeed, in presenting a strong and interesting argument, supported by a knowledge of the country under discussion very much greater than that possessed by his opponents, and a knowledge of events and larger issues not greatly, if at all, inferior to theirs. From what is now to be related, it appears that, decry him as they might, what he had written in his two books continued to vex them and to draw comment and argument from them in later writings.

One of the bitterest contemporary personal attacks upon Evans is that quoted in Stevens's *Lewis Evans*, 3d ed., page 13, in the form of a long, anonymous paragraph which Mr. Stevens found in manuscript attached to a copy of one of the London reprints of Evans's map. We are able to identify this unflattering comment as a copy of the note appended to pages 138–139 of William Smith's *History of New-York*, London, 1757. Fixing the authorship of this piece upon Smith ties it up with the New York group responsible for the *Review of the Military Operations*, London, 1757, for Smith was close to William Livingston and William Alexander, and has even been said, probably without truth, to have had a part in the authorship of the *Review*, another work in which Evans was traduced. The passage from the *Review of the Military Operations* is of such interest in an account of Evans and his work that it must be quoted in full. With a marginal note as its heading it is quoted below, with its footnotes, from pages 105–106 of that work:

HE PROCURES ONE EVANS TO PUBLISH INVECTIVES AGAINST THE GENERAL

This gentleman [i.e., Thomas Pownall], my Lord, became acquainted at Philadelphia with one Evans, who for a * valuable con-

---

* Among other gentlemen of distinction in the colonies, Mr. Pownal became acquainted with Mr. Alexander, of New York; a person of a friendly disposition and easy access. Mr. Alexander had now the surveyor general's office of New Jersey: and Mr. Pownal, to procure the fulsome dedication from Evans, promised him that office, upon his accession to the government. This, Evans frequently declared in his last illness to one of his most intimate friends; who concealed it till after his death. Such an anecdote will scarcely be credited by those unacquainted with Mr. Pownal's insatiable ambition to rise in America . . .

sideration, dedicated to him his map of the middle British colonies, with an encomium, that he esteemed him the best judge of it in America. This man having, in the public streets of Philadelphia, not only presumed to accuse Governor Morris of high treason, but to asperse two of his Majesty's ministers as pensioners to France, fled from justice there, and took sanctuary in New York, Mr. Morris however commenced an action against him in this province, more for his own vindication, than a reparation of damages; which the poor fellow would never have been able to make. Upon this he was committed to Gaol, till Mr. Oliver De Lancey so far befriended him, as to become his security. These were his circumstances, when he published a pamphlet full of invectives against General Shirley. I will not affirm, that he wrote it at the instance of the cabal in New York. I leave your Lordship to judge how far they were concerned in it, after adding, that it contained their repeated remarks; that Mr. Pownal was frequently at his lodgings about the time of its publication; and did actually accompany him to a printer, to hasten the impression, before he sailed for * England. I shall not trouble your

---

* Upon the news of the loss of Oswego, part of it was republished in the New York Gazette, to lead the populace to impute this calamity to General Shirley. It was appealed to, as an indisputable authority, by the very persons to whom poor Evans was indebted for his materials; and without whose dictating, it would never have seen the light. To write a book in another's name, and then to quote it as an authority, is a species of proof, with which Euclid appears to have been utterly unacquainted.

Lordship with any particular observations upon this libel. If ever it should fall into your Lordship's hands, this letter will assist you in detecting its falsehoods, and forming a proper judgment both of its author and his abettors.

Evans's map of 1755 and his *Geographical Essays* were well received in England. The map and the *Essays* [No. I] were reviewed in the *Monthly Review* for January, 1756, pages 29–37, and the *Essays No. II* in the same periodical for September, 1756, page 312. The first of these reviews which spoke of the "important Tendency" of the work, was written (Information from Benjamin C. Nangle of Yale University) by William Bewley, a regular reviewer for Griffiths's periodical. The authorship of the second is unknown. The *Gentleman's Magazine* for October, 1755, page 479, entered the map and the Dodsley issue of the first pamphlet among books published in October. The *Monthly Review* notices were favorable, but another which is of special interest to us, though favorable in the main, did not spare criticism of certain features of the book. Boswell puts it on record (*Life of Johnson*, I, 206,

Oxford ed., 1924) that Dr. Johnson reviewed Evans's map and the first pamphlet in the *Literary Magazine and Universal Review,* a periodical which he superintended and contributed to in the first year or so of its existence. Through the courtesy of the Yale University Library I have been supplied with a copy of the review of "Evans's Map and Account of the Middle English Colonies in America" which occupies pages 293–299, in Volume I of that magazine, being the number for September 15–October 15, 1756. Nearly five of the six pages are given up to quotation from the *Geographical Essays.* Certain paragraphs of the comment are of sufficient interest to quote here because they bespeak the importance of Evans's work in the juncture in which it appeared, and because Dr. Johnson, whether he express insular superiority, invincible ignorance, or incomparable good sense, and all three are combined in this review, is always good reading:

Nothing in this world is simply good. Peace the great blessing of the world, produces luxury, idleness and effeminacy. Scarcely any thing is simply evil. War among its numerous miseries has sometimes useful consequences. The last war between the Russians and Turks made Geographers acquainted with the situation and extent of many countries little known before, in the north of Europe, and the war now kindled in America, has incited us to survey and delineate the immense wastes of the western continent by stronger motives than mere science or curiosity could ever have supplied, and enabled the imagination to wander over the lakes and mountains of that region, which many learned men have marked as the seat destined by providence for the fifth empire.

At what time, or whether at any time their prediction will be verified, no human sagacity can discover, but as power is the constant and unavoidable consequence of learning, there is no reason to doubt that the time is approaching when the Americans shall in their turn have some influence on the affairs of mankind, for literature apparently gains ground among them. A library is established in Carolina; and some great electrical discoveries were made at Philadelphia, where the map and treatise which we are now about to consider were likewise printed and engraved.

> Westward the seat of empire takes its way,
> The four first acts already past,
> The fifth shall end the drama with the day,
> Time's noblest product is the last.
>
> Bp. Berkley.\

To this great event the present inland war cannot fail to contribute, as the inhabitants will necessarily become better versed in the military arts, and the Indians themselves as they are courted by one or other of the contending nations, will learn the use of European weapons, and the convenience of European institutions. They will at least in time learn their own importance, and will be incited to attempt something more than the chase of Beavers, when they are once convinced that something more may be performed.

The map is engraved with sufficient beauty, and the treatise written with such elegance as the subject admits tho' not without some mixture of the American dialect, a tract of corruption to which every language widely diffused must always be exposed. . . .

As this treatise consists principally of descriptions of roads disfigured by Indian names, and of authorities on which the map depends, it scarcely admits of extract or epitome. There are however interspersed some observations like green spots among barren mountains from which our readers will obtain a just idea of the situation and state of those untravelled countries. . . .

He concludes his pamphlet with some observations which may be of great use in the present system of European policy, but which will not prove that this system is right, or in other words, that it is more productive than any other of universal happiness. . . .

It is indeed supposed by our author to receive inhabitants from Europe; but we must remember that it will very little advance the power of the English to plant colonies on the Ohio by dispeopling their native country. And since the end of all human actions is happiness, why should any number of our inhabitants be banished from their trades and their homes to a trackless desart, where life is to begin anew, and where they can have no other accommodation, than their own hands shall immediately procure them. What advantage even upon supposition of, what is scarcely to be supposed, an uninterrupted possession and unimpeded improvement, can arise equivalent to the exile of the first planters, and difficulties to be encountered by their immediate descendants.

We have at home more land than we cultivate, and more materials than we manufacture; by proper regulations we may employ all our people, and give every man his chance of rising to the full enjoyment of all the pleasures and advantages of a civilised and learned country.

I know not indeed, whether we can at home procure any great

quantity of raw silk, which we are told is to be had in so great plenty upon the banks of the Ohio. Away therefore with thousands and millions to those dreadful desarts, that we may no longer want raw silk. Who that had not often observed how much one train of thought sometimes occupies the mind could think so wild a project seriously proposed?

The fear that the American colonies will break off their dependence on England, I have always thought, with this writer, chimerical and vain. Yet though he endeavours for his present purpose to shew the absurdity of such suspicions, he does not omit to hint at something that is to be feared if they are not well used. Every man and every society is intitled to all the happiness that can be enjoyed with the security of the whole community. From this general claim the Americans ought not to be excluded, but let us not be frightened by their threats, they must be yet dependent, and if they forsake us, or be forsaken by us, must fall into the hands of France.

APPENDIX VII

[WILLIAM LIVINGSTON], REVIEW OF THE MILITARY OPERATIONS IN NORTH AMERICA

---

1. A Review of the military Operations in North-America; from . . . 1753 to . . . 1756 . . . In a Letter to a Nobleman. London: Printed for R. and J. Dodsley in Pall-Mall. M.DCC.LVII.

    4to. [i–iv], 1–144. Dated at end, page 144: "New York, Sept. 20, 1756."

2. A Review of the military Operations in North America; . . . To which are added, Colonel Washington's Journal of his Expedition to the Ohio, in 1754, and several Letters and other Papers of Consequence, found in the Cabinet of Major General Braddock, after his Defeat near Fort Du Quesne; and since published by the French Court. [*cut of pointing hand*] None of these Papers are contained in the English Edition. Dublin: Printed for P. Wilson, and J. Exshaw, in Dame-Street. M,DCC,LVII.

    12mo. Pages 1–276. Page 1: title, verso blank; pages 3–190: text, headed "A Review of the military Operations in North America, &c."; pages 191–276: "Appendix.", comprising documents, numbered I–IX.

3. A Review of the military Operations in North-America, . . . London: Printed, for R. and J. Dodsley in Pall-Mall. M DCC LVII. New-England, Re-Printed in the Year. M,DCC,LVIII.

    Sm. 4to. Pages 1–98, including half-title. Dated at end as in No. 1 above.

4. A Review of the military Operations in North-America; . . . New-York: Printed by Alexander and James Robertson, MDCCLXX.

    8vo. Pages 1–170, including half-title. Dated at end, through error, "New York, Sept. 20, 1765," for 1756.

AUTHORSHIP OF THE TRACT

The authorship of the book is expressly attributed to William Livingston by Theodore Sedgwick, Jr., in his *Memoir of William Livingston* in a passage beginning on page 114. Referring in that passage to the republication of the book in the Massachusetts Historical Society *Collections*, for 1800, pages 67–163, Sedgwick proceeds:

"In this work Mr. Livingston is said, I know not on what authority, to have been assisted by William Smith and John Morine Scott. For the facts which it contains, he was probably in a considerable degree indebted to his brother-in-law, Mr. Alexander, afterwards Lord Stirling, who was about this time secretary to General Shirley; and agreeing, as he is known to have, with the two persons first named in their views of the politics of the province, it may be supposed that they took an interest, perhaps an active one, in its composition and progress, but the work as it now stands bears strong marks of being the production of a single hand. The internal evidence is indeed so complete, that even without the author's assertions, which are positive, I should consider it more probable that it was written by any one of the three already named, than by them conjointly." William Alexander's remarks to John Pownall quoted below suggest, too, a single individual as the author of the book, and claim that individual as his "particular friend at New York," words which he very well might use in speaking of his brother-in-law, William Livingston. One regrets that Mr. Sedgwick, the biographer, did not refer his readers to the place in which Livingston positively asserted his authorship of this book.

The *Colden Papers* (V, 157–159, Alexander Colden to Cadwallader Colden, New York, July 12, 1757) acquaint us with a picturesque incident in the history of the book:

By the Pacquet rec^d a letter from Mr Harison of the 14th May . . . He has Sent me a Pamphlet (which shall Send to you) he calls it a rare production of last Month as it was then published tho said to be wrote in New York some months ago. He desires me to let Mr Watts have it as soon as possible. Mr John Pownell brother to the Govr Waited upon Mr Alexander and he says he gives me their Dialogue Verbatim as he had it from an intimate of Mr Pownells & you will beleive it when I tell you Mr Alexander Confirmed it to me last Night in Vaux Hall Gardens—Thus then you have it

P. Sir I am informed that you are the Author of this piece which Contains many false and Scandalous Reflections upon my Brothers Character

A. Sir I am not the Author I assure you upon my Honor

P. Sir Did you not carry it to Dodsley the Printer and order'd him to publish it

A. I did Sir

P. I have it in my Power Sir by these minutes of Council from New Jersey to disprove such a particular thing

A. Sir I am convinced the Author is mistaken in that particular Instance, and as he is my particular friend at New York I will write to him and have it Cleared up which if he refuses to do I will give you his Name—

This is as nearly the Substance of what I heard as I can recollect, only that there was great Warmth on the Side of M͏ʳ Pownell, & as I told you above I met M͏ʳ Alex͏ʳ and Staats Morris last Night at Vaux Hall we went into an Alcove & drank a bottle of wine, when I took occasion to mention what I had heard & M͏ʳ Alexander assured me it was true, but that there was more which I had not heard and as you Capt͏ⁿ Morris was present I desire you will give M͏ʳ Harison an Acc͏ᵗ of it. Staats began thus. M͏ʳ Alex͏ʳ told M͏ʳ Pownell that tho he was not the Author yet he would prove every Article charged against his brother to be true, and a great deal more, and that he had, out of regard to him and his brothers Connections here forbid the Printer to publish Several passages of a much worse nature, but equally true, and which must have Set him in the most Contemptible light, & which can be proved by Hundreds of Witnesses, and in Short Sir Your brother, is a man not fitt to be intrusted, he is void even of common honesty, & capable of any thing.

NOTES ON THE EDITIONS

1. The *Review of the Military Operations*, full title in Sabin, No. 41649, is given place in the Register of Books published in the *Gentleman's Magazine* for May, 1757, page 242, but writing to Alexander Colden from London on May 14, 1757 (see above), George Harrison calls it "a rare production of last Month as it was then published."

2. The Dublin edition contains in addition to the *Review* a translation in sections, numbered I–VIII, of the material composing Nos. VIII–XV of the "Pièces Justificatives, Première Partie" of the *Mémoire contenant le Précis des Faits* issued by the French Government in 1756. (See Chapter II, note 48.) The Dublin book contains also one piece not found in the *Mémoire* in the form of its Number IX, headed "Copy of Major-General Johnson's Letter to the Governors of the Several Colonies." with date line, "Camp at Lake George, Sept. 9, 1755." This is a copy of Johnson's letter telling of the victory at Lake George published in America immediately after the

event. See Evans, No. 7441. (The John Carter Brown Library has this letter in two contemporary editions, of two leaves each, attributed respectively to New York and Newport.) The Dublin translation of the "Pièces Justificatives" is different from that found in the translation of the *Mémoire,* published in Philadelphia and New York in this year. (See Chapter II, notes 49–51.)

3. Evans, No. 8163, gives full title, suggesting New Haven as the place of publication. An examination of certain of the typographical ornaments employed at various places in the book shows them to be identical with some used by James Parker in other issues of his New Haven press. Though not conclusive evidence, this similarity in ornament gives strong support to Mr. Evans's attribution of the book to Parker's New Haven press. Trumbull, *List of Books Printed in Connecticut,* No. 1297, suggests Hartford as the place of publication of the book, but as it is well understood that printing did not begin at Hartford until the coming of Thomas Green in 1764, this must have been an inadvertency on the part of the Connecticut bibliographer. This "New England" edition seems to have been the only reprint of the book to issue from an American press at the time of its first publication.

4. Evans, No. 11701, gives full title of this late New York edition of a book first published in 1757. No one seems to have attempted an explanation of the reprinting of this book in New York in 1770, long after the military conduct of General Shirley had ceased to be of importance. A possible explanation, however, lies in the fact that in this year Livingston's animosities were brought to the surface again through his defeat at the polls, the year before, by the conservative interests of New York. One form his revenge took was the writing and publishing in this year of the *Soliloquy,* a savage attack upon Governor Cadwallader Colden and his associates. He may well have thought that the republication of the *Review* with its attacks upon the De Lancey–Sir William Johnson–Pownall group would provide further justification of his career of liberalism. Proposals for publication by subscription, dated "New-York, February 22, 1770," found in the *Newport Mercury* for April 23, 1770, give the following explanation of the republication of the book at this time:

> "N.B. This Book was published in London, Anno 1757, and the Sale of it in England was so rapid, that very few Copies came to America, and those were instantly bought up, so that several

Gentlemen who are desirous of perusing this valuable and curious Performance, have not had the Opportunity of purchasing it."

CONTEMPORARY COMMENT

William Smith, Jr., *History of New York*, ed. of 1830, II, 311, wrote of the *Review of the Military Operations* (see Sedgwick's *Memoir*, page 117, for this correct condensation of Smith's actual words): "No reply was ever made to this pamphlet; coming out when America was little known, and transactions here still less, it was universally read and talked of in London, and worked consequences of private and public utility. General Shirley emerged from a load of obloquy. His extensive designs acquired advocates; his successors became cautious and vigilant; party-spirit less assuming, and the multitude so enlightened, that several changes were made on the next dissolution." This complacent encomium of a book of the author's own faction is counterbalanced by the opening sentences of the notice that Oliver Goldsmith wrote of it in the *Monthly Review* for June, 1757, page 524: "Though the Author of this letter sets out with assuring the nameless Peer, to whom it is addressed, of his impartiality, yet by his vindication of every measure that Governor Shirley undertook, and by his censure of almost every measure in which this Gentleman was not concerned, we are too much led to suspect him of having an interested attachment to one party, implicitly to believe all he says against the other." And later in the same notice, page 527: ". . . the Author's chief design, is to vindicate Mr. Shirley, and asperse the characters of those who opposed his measures. Upon the whole, he seems too warm, to have all the weight which he may wish to have with his readers."

APPENDIX VIII

SAMUEL HAZARD'S COLONY AND
HIS PRINTED SCHEME

1. Scheme for the Settlement of a new Colony to the Westward of Pennsylvania, for the Enlargement of his Majesty's Dominions in America, for the further Promotion of the Christian Religion among the Indian Natives, and for the more effectual Securing them in his Majesty's Alliance.

   Single leaf, printed both sides, measuring approximately 8 × 13 inches. Recto: heading as above, followed by text of *Scheme*, concluding with paragraph beginning "That the Indians shall . . ."; verso: two paragraphs of text, followed by "To the Honourable the Governor, Council and Representatives of the Colony of Connecticut, to meet in General Assembly, on the Eighth Day of May, 1755. The Petition of the Subscribers, being Inhabitants of His Majesty's Plantations in North-America, Humbly Sheweth:", followed by text of the Petition in 32 lines. (Connecticut State Library, Connecticut Archives, Susquehannah Settlers, 1775–1796, Vol. I. doc. 2.)

2. Scheme for the Settlement . . . [*heading with wording as above*].
   Single leaf, printed both sides, measuring approximately 8½ × 14½ inches. Recto: heading, followed by entire text of *Scheme*; verso: "To his Majesty George the Second, by the Grace of God of Great Britain, France, and Ireland, King Defender of the Faith, and so forth. The Humble Address of Persons, Inhabitants of his Majesty's Plantations in North America. May it Please your Majesty.", followed by text of the address in three paragraphs, and at the end "Dated at Philadelphia, July 24th, 1755." (Connecticut State Library, 2 copies: Trumbull Papers, 23.8, formerly in Massachusetts Historical Society; and Susquehannah Settlers, 1775–1796, Vol. I. doc. 54.)

   Franklin to Collinson, June 26, 1755, Smyth, *Writings of Benjamin Franklin*, III, 265–266: "There is one Mr. Hazard, who, happening to see last Fall a Paper of mine on the Means of settling a new Colony westward of Pensilvania (drawn up to divert the Connecticut Emigrants from their design of Invading this Province and so induce them to go where they would be less injurious and more useful) and picking out something farther from me in Conversation, has publish'd a Scheme for that purpose in my Absence, wherein he has added some Things and left out others, and now (like your Fire-hearth Man) calls it his own Project. He aims at great Matters for himself, hoping to become a Proprietor like Mr. Penn etc. and has got, they say, a great Number of Settlers engag'd to go with him, if he can get a grant of the Land from the Crown. It is certain that People enough may be had, to make a strong English Settlement or two in those Parts. I wish to see it done; yet I think this Man not the fittest in the World to conduct such an Affair. I hear he intends soon for England."

The "Paper" on this subject that Franklin refers to as having been seen by Mr. Hazard in the fall of 1754 is printed in Smyth, *Writings of Benjamin Franklin*, III, 358–366. It is entitled "Plan for Settling two Western Colonies in North America, with Reasons for the Plan."

On April 4, 1755 (*V & P of the Pennsylvania Assembly*, Miller ed., IV, 394), Mr. Samuel Hazard petitioned the House for assistance in carrying out the scheme he had projected for the settlement of a new colony to the westward of Pennsylvania, such a colony, he averred, being "highly necessary for the Safety of this and all his Majesty's Colonies in North-America, and would be of very great Advantage to the Trade of Great-Britain." The petition was laid on the table, and on June 25th a letter to the Speaker from Samuel Hazard concerning his petition was read and in its turn "Ordered to lie on the Table." It was probably the state of the country and the defeat soon afterwards of Braddock that made discussion of this petition seem undesirable at that time, for it did not leave the table again that session. Hazard, however, was not discouraged by the conditions, for the address to the King attached to one edition of his printed *Scheme*, No. 2, above, is dated July 24th, some days after the news of Braddock's defeat had reached Philadelphia.

Hazard's proposal was to occupy a tract west of Pennsylvania belonging by charter right to the colony of Connecticut, and on May 8, 1755 (*American Archives*, 4th Ser. I, 863–864), he personally petitioned the Connecticut Assembly to release to him its claim to the lands he intended to settle, saying, among many other things, that he had already engaged 3,508 settlers. The favorable reply of the Connecticut Assembly is found in full in the *Pennsylvania Archives*, II, 301–302, with a footnote to Samuel Hazard's name reading, "Grandfather of the

Editor," i.e., of Samuel Hazard, editor of the *Pennsylvania Archives*. It is found, too, in *American Archives*, 4th Ser. I, 864–865. Sometime in the months before this action was taken Hazard had circulated the printed *Scheme* described in No. 1, above, with its petition addressed to the Connecticut Assembly convening May 8 by subscribers throughout the colonies. After the petition had been granted by the Connecticut legislators, a new edition of the *Scheme* was brought out (No. 2 above), in which the petition to the Assembly was replaced by an address to the King. In 1774 Ebenezer Hazard, son of Samuel, petitioned the Connecticut Assembly for a confirmation of his father's claim. The prayer of Ebenezer's memorial, however, was not granted. The papers in the Connecticut Archives relating to this scheme have been printed in *American Archives*, as cited above, and in the *Susquehanna Company Papers*, edited by Julian B. Boyd. (Wyoming Historical and Geological Society, 3v., Wilkes-Barre, 1930.)

It is by no means certain that the two editions of the *Scheme* entered here represent all the contemporaneous printed documents issued by Hazard, but they are all that I have found. It probably was the *Scheme* entered above as No. 1, issued before May 8, 1755, that Franklin referred to in his letter to Collinson of June 26th as having been published during his recent absence, which had lasted, roughly, from September 1, 1754, until March 1, 1755. Neither of these pieces has been previously noticed by bibliographers, though their content has been available to historians in the publications of later date mentioned above. No. 1 forms part of the records in the Connecticut Archives relating to the Hazard proposal. A photostat copy has been courteously supplied me by Mr. George S. Godard, librarian of the Connecticut State Library. No. 2 (Trumbull Papers, 23.8) came into the possession of the Connecticut State Library, when some years ago these papers were generously turned over to it by the Massachusetts Historical Society. The second copy of No. 2, mentioned above, that found in Connecticut Archives, Susquehannah Settlers, 1775–1796, I, 54, bears the manuscript note on its face, "Accompanying Hazard's petition," and is doubtless the copy of the *Scheme* submitted by Ebenezer Hazard when, in 1174, he petitioned the Connecticut Assembly for confirmation of his father's privileges. Photostat copies of both pieces are in the John Carter Brown Library. It is clear that No. 1 is an early form of the *Scheme*, as printed, for the clause on lines 3 and 4 of the text, "to extend from the western boundaries of Pennsylvania," has been altered with a pen to read, "to begin at a distance of one Hundred Miles Westward of ye Western bounds of Pennsylvania, and thence to extend . . ." This corrected version of the clause was necessitated by the Connecticut Assembly's amendment of the *Scheme.* The correction is printed in the text of No. 2. In his *Susquehanna Company Papers,* I, 251–259, Mr. Boyd prints a combination of the two editions of the *Scheme,* our Nos. 1 and 2, with the heading: "Broadside of Samuel Hazard's Scheme for a New Colony," thus creating a document that seems never to have existed. It is certainly not found among the papers in the Connecticut Archives to which he specifically refers.

APPENDIX IX

[WILLIAM DOUGLASS], A SUMMARY HISTORICAL AND POLITICAL, OF THE BRITISH SETTLEMENTS IN NORTH-AMERICA

Richardson, *Early American Magazines*, pages 57–58, cites the proposals in the *American Magazine and Historical Chronicle* for January, 1746, in which was announced the proposed publication by installments of Douglass's *Summary* in that periodical. There was, however, a subsequent change of plan by which, beginning in 1747, the *Summary* was separately issued, irregularly as to time, in parts of 16 pages each, with covers of the same paper, comprising title and 3 pages of printed advertisements. Parts 1–36 of Volume I appeared in the years 1747–1749, and were combined, with covers removed, into a single volume by Rogers & Fowle with a title-page dated 1749. Parts 1–26 of Volume II were issued separately in the same manner from 1750–1752. No. 26, dated on cover "1751," carries on the inside front cover the notice of Douglass's death in October, 1752, but the date 1752 does not appear on the covers of any of these parts. The parts were now combined, with covers removed, and issued as Volume II, but the title-page of the volume still bore the date 1751. The first combined edition of the work, therefore, bears the dates 1749 and 1751, for Volumes I and II respectively, though the actual date of publication of Volume II was 1752. In 1755 the first London edition of the book appeared with imprint as follows: "Boston, New-England, Printed: London, reprinted for R. Baldwin in Pater-noster-Row. M.DCC.LV." The map "North America From the French of Mr. D'Anville . . ." published by Thomas Jefferys in May, 1755, that accompanies this edition is the first appearance of a map in connection with the book. The note to this edition in Sabin, No. 20727, seems to be taken from a clipping pasted on the fly-leaf of the John Carter Brown copy, but the clipping itself and a note in John Carter Brown's hand make it clear that the statement there made; that is, that the map was never found in the book in its original state refers, not to the edition of 1755, but to that of 1760. The statement should be disregarded altogether, however, for it is incorrect also with regard to the edition of 1760 (London, Printed for R. and J. Dodsley, in Pall-mall. MDCCLX). As explained in our Appendix III, copies of this edition of 1760 in the New York Public Library (3 copies alike), the American Antiquarian Society, and in the Library of Congress, contain the Huske "Map of North America" which Dodsley originally printed in 1755 to accompany the proposed but never published Part II of John Huske's *Present State of North America*. The Jefferys map in the *Summary* of London, 1755, mentioned above, also made a reappearance in 1760 in Jefferys's own work, *The natural and civil History of the French Dominions in North and South America*.

These are the main features of the editions of Douglass's *Summary*. It has not been possible for me to make at this time a thorough bibliographical study of the book, with its original issues in parts and its various consolidated issues and editions. See Evans, Nos. 5936, 6126, 6306, 6490, 6662, 6663, 6992, and 7885, also Sabin, Nos. 20726–20728.

APPENDIX X

[CADWALLADER COLDEN], THE HISTORY OF THE FIVE INDIAN NATIONS

1. The History of the Five Indian Nations depending on the Province of New-York in America. Printed and Sold by William Bradford in New-York, 1727.

   Sm. 8vo. Pages [i–ii], I–XVIII, 1–119.

2. The History of the Five Indian Nations of Canada Which are dependent on the Province of New-York in America, . . . London: Printed for T. Osborne in Gray's-Inn. MDCCXLVII.

   8vo. Pages i–xvi, [i–iv], 1–90, i–iv, 91–204; 1–283, [284]. Map.

3. The History of the Five Indian Nations of Canada, which are the Barrier between the English and French. . . . The second Edition. London: Printed for John Whiston at Mr. Boyle's Head, and Lockyer Davis at Lord Bacon's Head, both in Fleet-street, and John Ward opposite the Royal Exchange. MDCCL.

   8vo. Pages [i–ii], i–xvi, [i–iv], 1–90, i–iv, 91–204; 1–283, [284]; Map. Page [i]: blank; page [ii], facing title: book advertisement. The Contents, 2 leaves, here described as [i–iv] are, in the John Carter Brown copy, bound between pages x and xi. Sabin says some copies are undated.

4. The History of the Five Indian Nations of Canada, Which are dependent On the Province of New-York in America, . . . In two Volumes. The third Edition. London: Printed for Lockyer Davis, at Lord Bacon's Head in Fleet-street; J. Wren in Salisbury-court; and J. Ward in Cornhill, opposite the Royal-Exchange. MDCCLV.

   12mo. Pages i–xii, [i–iv], 1–260; [i–iv], 1–251, [252–260]; Map. Pages [252–260]: books advertised by Lockyer Davis, J. Wren, and J. Ward, separately.

GENERAL STATEMENT

One of the best bibliographical studies of a single book published in the United States in the nineteenth century, or since, is the Introduction affixed by John Gilmary Shea to his reprint of the first edition, New York, 1727, of Colden's *History of the Five Indian Nations*. One is hardly able to add an essential fact to Dr. Shea's history of the book in its several editions, but it is possible to produce some additional illustrative material bearing upon several points briefly touched in that Introduction. This has been made easy by the publication of the *Letters and Papers of Cadwallader Colden*, 1711–1775, 7 v., New York, 1918–1923, in the "Collections of the New York Historical Society," a group of documents of the first importance in the history of the period they cover. The indexes of Volumes II, III, and IV will direct the reader to many references to Colden's *History* not cited or quoted here.

NOTES ON THE EDITIONS

1. *The History of the Five Indian Nations, With an Introduction and Notes By John Gilmary Shea*, New York, 1866, gives a page-by-page reprint of this edition. Its full title is given above, in Sabin, No. 14270, and in Evans, No. 2849. Sabin's note to No. 14270, however, confuses the work with the *Papers Relating to the Indian Trade* of 1724, his No. 14272, when it records that the publication of the *History, etc.* "was occasioned by a dispute between the government of New York and some merchants, and is mainly a legal argument." Evans, also, No. 2512, describing the *Papers, etc.*, of 1724, calls it "The first edition of Colden's History of the Five Nations." These two works, however, are entirely distinct. As explained below under (2), their first association was when the *Papers* was added as a separate section to the London, 1747, edition of the *History*.

No. 1, above, the true first edition of Colden's *History, etc.*, was advertised as "just published" in the *New York Gazette* for March 13, 1726/27. As appears from a letter of Colden to Collinson of December, 1743 (*Colden Papers*, III, 42–45), 500 copies of this edition were printed and all were sold. For a discussion of this first edition, especially the conclusion that it does not rightly have with it the "Map of the Country of the Five Nations" of 1724, a reissue of which Bradford advertised in the *History* itself, page xviii, see V. H. Paltsits in Stokes, *Iconography of Manhattan Island*, VI, 259–260. It may be observed that the statement there made to the effect that 300 copies of the book were printed is contradicted by Colden's own assertion just referred to, that 500 copies had been printed and sold.

2. A full title and collation of the book are given in Shea, work cited above, pages xvi–xix. See also Sabin, No. 14273. From the sense of the letters of Collinson and Osborne of March 27 and June 12, 1747 (*Colden Papers*, III, 369–370, 402–403), respectively, one concludes that the book was published between these dates, and from Osborne's letter of June 6, 1748 (*Colden Papers*, IV, 64–66), it appears that the edition consisted of 1000 copies.

The first intimation that exists of Peter Collinson's interest in seeing a new and revised edition of the book, mentioned by Dr. Shea, is found in his letter to Colden of March 5, 1740/41 (*Colden Papers*, II, 207–208). Collinson writes: "Wee are in hopes you will oblige the Curious wth the other p^{t} of the Histo^{y} of the Five Nations . . . and if you don't choose to print it y^{r} self there is those in London will Readly do It and as the First part is quite out of print, what if It Suffer a Revisal or Aditions & Both come out together . . ." Collinson's suggestion is of interest in view of the fact that it was exactly this form the edition of 1747 took. In reply to this suggestion, Colden, writing probably in May, 1741, according to the rough draft remaining (*Colden Papers*, II, 210–211), promised to revise and enlarge the book, and less than a year later, on April 9, 1742 (*Colden Papers*, II, 250–251), he sent Collinson "the greatest part the Indian History continued to the peace of Reswick." Sometime in May, 1742 (*Colden Papers*, II, 257–263), he sent the remainder of the manuscript, and with it a letter of some length in which he admits with great modesty his shortcomings as an historian of the Indians, and relates for Collinson's private information much that he feared to include in the *History* "as it must throw severe reflections upon particular persons or families now in this Province."

In a letter of September 3, 1742 (*Colden Papers*, II, 271–272), Collinson acknowledged receipt of the manuscript. There seems to have been difficulty in procuring a publisher who would undertake the work at his own expense, despite Collinson's initial assurance on this point. It is probable that the war with France that soon ensued forced Collinson to lay aside for some years the thought of finding a publisher for the book, but he did not completely lose sight of his purpose in that time. On March 27, 1747 (*Colden Papers*, III, 369–370), we find him writing Colden that the Indian history was now in press, that Mr. Osborne, the bookseller, had undertaken it at his own expense, that Dr. John Mitchell had helped compose its title-page, and that he, for his part, had "spared no thought or pains to Introduce it into the World at this Juncture when it was of such Importance to be perused by every True Lover of his Country." On June 12, 1747 (*Colden Papers*, III, 402–403), Colden learned from Osborne, the publisher, that the book was printed and copies on the way to America. A letter from Collinson of August 3, 1747 (*Colden Papers*, III, 410), explained that the change of dedication from Burnet to Oglethorpe had been made by Osborne without his knowledge or consent.

The initial reception of the *History* in London from the bookseller's standpoint was encouraging. On June 6, 1748 (*Colden Papers*, IV, 64), Osborne communicated to Colden the following details: "The Book was received in the World with the greatest Reputation; But I find in most Books after there has been a Run of about two or three hundred, that it drops off but slowly, which is the Case of this, for I have Actually not sold above three hundred, and two hundred which I have sent Abroad to different places which I have no Account yett of the Sale off, So that I have Actually by me near 500 Books, Yet they drop off every now & then; I will take care & pay your compliments to Gen¹ Oglethorpe." But Osborne's tone was soon to change. Sometime in the next two years he sold the remainder of the edition and his rights in it to another publisher, and finally reported his reasons for doing so in a belated letter to Colden of June 20, 1751 (*Colden Papers*, IV, 270–271), in which he wrote as follows: "Sʳ I have Receiv'd the favour of both yours & Should have Answer'd the first before but that was upon so melancholy a Subject that I deferr'd writing as you will find hereafter Its True that I did inform you that the Indian History was well receiv'd, but for what Reason I cannot tell the Sale of it fell off before I sold one Quarter of the Impression and the Demand has been So very Smal ever Since That I was Glad to dispose of them at any Rate and what I had remaining upon my hands. I sold for Twelve Pence a Book, so that I am a Loser by that undertaking at least Thirty pounds Therefore I cannot give Encouragement to continue it on I shall be proud of Serving you with any Thing that I have but am determined for the future to Trade for nothing but ready money by which means I can afford to Sell cheaper than another."

The first appended section following Part II of the book is a reprint of the *Papers Relating to the Indian Trade* of New York, 1724, accompanied by a letter, pages 42–44, of "New York, 1740" from J. A. to P. C. From Colden's letter to Collinson of December,

1743 (*Colden Papers*, III, 42–45), we learn with certainty what we might have guessed as to these initials, namely that a copy of the *Papers* had been sent Collinson some years before by James Alexander of New York. Colden now suggested the addition to the *History* by way of appendix of that earlier compilation he had edited, containing, in addition to the collection of official papers, his own "Memorial concerning the Furr-Trade." This whole letter is of first-rate interest in the history of Colden's book and of his motives in its publication at this critical time.

The map found in this edition of the *History* of 1747 is a reduced copy, $6\frac{3}{16} \times 8\frac{15}{16}$ inches, of the famous "Map of the Country of the Five Indian Nations" which may have been drawn by Colden and was certainly engraved for and published with his *Papers Relating to the Indian Trade* of New York, 1724. It was reissued as a separate map without change in 1727, and reissued again with revisions and additions as a separate map in 1735. The original map of 1724 is reproduced, from the copy of the *Papers, etc.* belonging to the New York Public Library, in Stokes, *Iconography of Manhattan Island*, III, A. Plate 2 b. The map and its reissues are described in the same work, III, 862, but especially in V. H. Paltsits's bibliographical notes in VI, 259–260. The copy of the map in the London editions of the book is without name of engraver.

3. After the sale of the remainder sheets of the edition of 1747 as told by Osborne in his belated letter of June 20, 1751, quoted under (2) above, the purchasers brought out in 1750 this second issue of that edition, with a change in title (compare Sabin, Nos. 14273 and 14274), a different imprint, of course, and the words "The second Edition" on the title-page. This reissue embodies the same sheets with the exception of two leaves at the beginning containing a book advertisement and a new title in place of the canceled title of 1747. The verso of the new leaf facing the title contains a book advertisement of the new publishers, Whiston and Davis. Its collation otherwise is exactly that of No. 2, above. The new publishers even retained the final leaf of the edition of 1747, containing on its verso the advertisement of Osborne's recent publications. From Osborne's letters to Colden of June 6, 1748, and June 20, 1751, one judges that the remainder consisted of 500 copies, or under. The price at which it was sold to the new publishers, 12d a copy, seems extraordinarily small until differences in the value of money between then and now are taken in consideration. For comment upon its map, printed from the same plate as used in 1747, see section above (2).

4. It is evident that the combination of booksellers that issued (3) above found Colden's *History* a better selling book than it had proven itself to be in Osborne's hands. This is at least true of two of them, Lockyer Davis and John Ward, for when American affairs began to become acute again a few years later, these publishers joined to themselves J. Wren and published what they called "The third Edition," a complete resetting of type in twelvemo format in two volumes. The "Map of the Country of the Five Nations" is the only vestige in this edition of the edition of 1747. That map is from the original plate first used in Nos. 2 and 3, above described.

AN AMERICAN BOOKSHELF 1755

INDEX

(This index comprises the names of books, authors, and individuals
discussed in the text and Appendices.)